Praise for
The Social Compass Curriculum: A Story-Based Intervention Package for Students with Autism Spectrum Disorders

"An instructional curriculum that will enhance the lives of children with autism and those on the spectrum. This is a must-have curriculum for teachers!"
—Belinda Dunnick Karge, Ph.D., Director, Project AIMS: Autism, Inclusion, Math and Science, California State University

"Ideal for the busy school-based clinician or behaviorist . . . This is an excellent resource for use with our school-age ASD students."
—Michelle Garcia Winner, M.A., CCC-SLP, speech-language pathologist and Founder of Social Thinking

"Teachers and students can learn and benefit from this eminently doable curriculum."
—**Eliza DelPizzo-Cheng, Ph.D., BCBA-D,** IN STEPPS: Support, Treatment, & Education for Parents, Professionals, and Students

"I have witnessed numerous children develop strong social skills with the help of *The Social Compass Curriculum*. Finally, students from all over the world will be able to use what we in Southern California have had for years through this excellent guide."
—Gillian Hayes, Ph.D., Associate Professor, Donald Bren School of Information & Computer Sciences, University of California, Irvine

"A wonderful addition to the resource library of special educators . . . I will certainly include this in my Social Skills library!"
—Cindy Golden, Ed.D., Principal/Psychologist of NorthStar Educational and Therapeutic Services; author of *The Special Educator's Toolkit*; editor of *Special Needs Resource Magazine*

"An evidence-based intervention that is very user-friendly . . . emphasizes understanding of social interactions by contextualizing complex ideas in stories. A highly recommended book."
—Lauren Franke, Psy.D., CCC-SLP, speech-language pathologist and clinical psychologist

"A very useful resource for teaching social skills to students with autism spectrum disorders . . . will guide teachers in how to teach these elusive skills in concrete, fun, and interactive ways."
—Mary Jane Weiss, Ph.D., Professor and Director, Autism and Applied Behavior Analysis Program, Endicott College

THE SOCIAL COMPASS CURRICULUM

A Story-Based Intervention Package for Students with Autism Spectrum Disorders

THE SOCIAL COMPASS CURRICULUM

A Story-Based Intervention Package for Students with Autism Spectrum Disorders

by

LouAnne Boyd, M.A., BCBA

Christina McReynolds, Ed.S., M.S., BCBA

and

Karen Chanin, M.S., P.P.S.

North Orange County Special Education Local Plan Area
California

PAUL H. BROOKES PUBLISHING CO.®

Baltimore • London • Sydney

·P A U L·H·
BROOKES
PUBLISHING CO.®

Paul H. Brookes Publishing Co.
Post Office Box 10624
Baltimore, MD 21285-0624

www.brookespublishing.com

Typeset by Cenveo Publisher Services, Columbia, Maryland.
Manufactured in the United States of America by
Sheridan Books, Inc., Chelsea, Michigan.

Icons by Jan Schrieber, Graphic Muse Design.
Drawings by Nathan Smith.

Stock #: 74012
ISBN 13: 978-1-59857-401-2
ISBN 10: 1-59857-401-9

Sold as part of *The Social Compass Curriculum: A Story-Based Intervention Package for Students with Autism Spectrum Disorders*
Stock #: 72957
ISBN 13: 978-1-59857-295-7
ISBN 10: 1-59857-295-4

Library of Congress Cataloging-in-Publication Data

Boyd, LouAnne.
The social compass curriculum : a story-based intervention package for students with autism spectrum disorders / by LouAnne Boyd, M.A., BCBA, Christina McReynolds, Ed.S., M.S., BCBA, and Karen Chanin, M.S., P.P.S., North Orange County Special Education Local Plan Area California.
pages cm
Includes bibliographical references and index.
ISBN-13: 978-1-59857-401-2 (pbk.)
ISBN-10: 1-59857-401-9 (pbk.)
1. Autistic children—Education. 2. Autistic children—Education—Curricula. 3. Children with autism spectrum disorders. I. Title.

LC4717.B68 2013
371.9—dc23 2013001700

British Library Cataloguing in Publication data are available from the British Library.

2017 2016 2015 2014 2013

10 9 8 7 6 5 4 3 2 1

CONTENTS

About the Material Included in This Curriculum vi
Foreword *Peter F. Gerhardt* vii
About the Authors ix
Acknowledgments x

Introduction 1

Module 1: Nonverbal Skills 9
- Lesson 1A Body Language/Gestures 11
- Lesson 1B Space and Proximity 15
- Lesson 1C Volume of Voice 19
- Lesson 1D Social Referencing 23

Module 2: Emotions 27
- Lesson 2A Increasing Emotional Vocabulary 29
- Lesson 2B Identifying Intensity of Feelings 33
- Lesson 2C Empathy 37
- Lesson 2D Positive Self-Talk 41

Module 3: Social Problem Solving 45
- Lesson 3A Staying on Topic 47
- Lesson 3B Paying Attention 51
- Lesson 3C Accepting Change in Routines 55
- Lesson 3D Resisting Tattling 59
- Lesson 3E Handling Teasing 63
- Lesson 3F Using Self-Control 67
- Lesson 3G Avoiding Being Left Out 71

Module 4: "We" Skills 75
- Lesson 4A Initiating a Conversation 77
- Lesson 4B Asking Questions 81
- Lesson 4C Sharing Information 85
- Lesson 4D Giving Compliments 89
- Lesson 4E Expanding Personal Interests 93
- Lesson 4F Paraphrasing 97
- Lesson 4G Negotiating Needs 101
- Lesson 4H Maintaining a Conversation 105
- Lesson 4I Ending a Conversation 109

Appendix A: Photocopiable Materials for Use in Multiple Lessons 115
Appendix B: Lesson-Specific Resources 121

Index 177

ABOUT THE MATERIAL INCLUDED IN THIS CURRICULUM

The Social Compass Curriculum comes with all of the material needed to get started.

- **Reproducibles:** The appendixes at the end of this book (pp. 115–176) contain all worksheets and handouts for use with students and parents. Appendix A includes items used across more than one lesson (a Social Compass Icons Overview that students can use for reference and Reading Comprehension Sheets, which are the same for each lesson within a given module). Appendix B includes lesson-specific worksheets and handouts. **Need printable versions of the materials in this book?** Electronic versions of selected materials from this book are available on our web site. You can download and print them for free as you need them. Please visit www.brookespublishing.com/downloads and enter code 26ydLuW5r to access these materials.
- **Flashcards:** Bundled with this book is a set of full-color flashcards; there is one flashcard for each lesson's visual support icon. The reverse of each card includes an explanation of the icon and the key concept addressed. These flashcards can be used in the lessons and as reminders throughout a student's day.
- **Poster:** Also bundled with this book is a large full-color poster of the visual support icons, to be hung in the classroom as a reference. The poster will help remind students of the skills they learn throughout this curriculum for navigating social situations.

FOREWORD

What exactly are social skills? Are they primarily verbal skills (Could you pass the salt please?)? Are good social skills defined by your intent (I wanted to become part of the group, so I said, "Good morning gentlemen") or by their interpretation (What's up with the "gentlemen" thing? That's kinda odd)? How come social skills that work very well in one context (say, a Star Trek convention) are ineffective, or worse, offensive in another (a funeral)? And what exactly are roles of personal space, body posture, hand gestures, voice inflection and tone, humor, and sarcasm? What are the social rules about interacting with strangers, acquaintances, friends, family members, and lovers? What exactly are social skills?

Social skills, at least as I have come understand them, are our access and navigation skills. They are how we get things we want and avoid things we don't want. They allow us to play as part of a baseball team and excuse ourselves from situations that make us uncomfortable. A commonality of all useful social skills is that they help us achieve both short-term goals (having the salt passed to you) and long-term goals (celebrating a 50th anniversary). We acquire and maintain our repertoire of social skills because they, over time, have been reinforced by the preferred response of others. So if I want you to like me, I will use my polite and engaging set of social skills in hopes that that will come true. If I don't care if you like me, I will use a limited set of social skills, trusting that you will not find me interesting. If I don't like you and don't want you to like me, I will be, at best, noncommittal and, at worst, rude. Whichever set I use, I am getting the response I want, so these skills are reinforced and remain in my repertoire.

We humans, like many other inhabitants of this planet, are social beings, so from birth our brain is wired to allow us to, well, be social. Social opportunities are all around us, as are the associated social demands. In fact, if two people are in a shared space, it is impossible for us not to engage socially on some level (ignoring the person is social behavior). Some of what we do may be verbal, but the extent to which that is appropriate would depend on a number of factors. These factors, taken together, are known as context.

Perhaps more so than any other skill domain, social skills are tied to the context in which they are used. For example, learn to drive (an adaptive skill) and you can drive most anywhere in most any vehicle. Learn to ask someone if they have put on weight and there are only a few situations with a limited number of people where that would be considered endearing. Context can also turn a skill that is not considered to be a social skill into a social skill. Undress yourself in your room in preparation for going to bed and that is an adaptive life skill. Undress yourself self in a crowded elevator and now you have a social faux pas. Same skill. Different context. Different result.

To further complicate things, social skills have an exceedingly broad range of expression that is likely to be effective or, conversely, ineffective. Think for a moment of how many different ways there are to greet someone. Included are small gestures (waves, head nods), physical contact (hugs, kisses, fist bumps), monosyllabic vocalizations (Yo, Hey, Hi), multisyllabic vocalizations (Hello, How's it going), and any number of combinations as a function of your relationship with the person and the physical context of the greeting. And the wrong combination in the wrong context can be embarrassing, uncomfortable, and even illegal (e.g., kissing and hugging someone who does not want to be hugged).

So social skills are complex, contextual-based skills that we neurotypicals, given our neurological make-up, acquire easily and use almost effortlessly. Individuals on the autism spectrum, however, experience social skills very differently. Start with difficulties understanding basic social communication (let alone challenges in interpreting social nuance); add to that the skill complexity—including context variables—that defines social competence; insert questions as to the reinforcement different individuals on the spectrum may find in social interaction; and we have, at least from the point of view of intervention, a perfect storm.

All of which leads me to *The Social Compass Curriculum: A Story-Based Intervention Package for Students with Autism Spectrum Disorders,* by LouAnne Boyd, M.A., BCBA, Christina McReynolds, Ed.S., M.S., BCBA, and Karen Chanin, M.S., PPS. *The Social Compass Curriculum* recognizes the complexity of social skills and the challenges associated with their instruction that is, in and of itself, noteworthy. Going further, however, Boyd and colleagues have put forth an instructional model that is systematic, uses established interventions, and puts a high priority on generalization and maintenance of acquired skills outside of the context of instruction.

Now, if you are interested in *The Social Compass Curriculum* because you think it will solve all of your instructional challenges in the area of social skills with individuals on the autism spectrum, I have some bad news for you. It won't. Social skills are not that simple, and neither is social skills instruction. That is why I like Boyd and colleagues' overall formulation of the program as a *compass*. First, a compass in the hands of an untrained navigator is a pretty, but overall useless, instrument. The same is true with the Social Compass in that a general understanding of data-based intervention with individuals with autism is a the base of its effective implementation. Second, being able to read a compass accurately absent the ability to then navigate in the right direction is, once again, a useless skill. Although the practices and protocols contained herein will point you in the right direction, the skills targeted need to be taught, assessed, taught, assessed, taught, assessed, and, then, generalized under your direction. Finally, the knowledgeable use of a compass and an understanding of navigation also allows you to change directions during storms, low tides, floods, and so forth. The same, I believe, is true here. When faced with slow skill acquisition, you need to determine the cause and remediate. When face with no, or limited, generalization, you may need to modify your teaching skills to in order to provide more effective instruction. Let's face it—even the most experienced navigator makes a wrong turn from time to time. The best ones, however, figure out the mistake and correct their course. That—whether you are a teacher, a speech pathologist, a behavior analyst, or a parent—is your responsibility here. So take this Social Compass and, with all the determination and skill you bring to the table, use it to help your students get pointed in the right social direction.

Peter F. Gerhardt, Ed.D.
Director of Education
Upper School of the McCarton School, New York
Founding Chair, Scientific Council
Organization for Autism Research

ABOUT THE AUTHORS

LouAnne Boyd, M.A., BCBA, is a private practitioner and the owner of ABAcus: Behavioral Tools for Social Engagement. In addition, she is Autism Coordinator for the North Orange County Special Education Local Plan Area in California. LouAnne conducts social skills groups in her community for both students with autism and neurotypical children. She conducts staff and parent trainings for social, communication, and behavioral interventions for home and school. LouAnne teaches graduate-level courses for in-service special educators focused on evidence-based interventions in the classroom at California State University, Fullerton. Since the early 1990s, she has served in clinic, community, and school settings. Her current interests include assessment, intervention, and generalization of social skills training.

Christina McReynolds, Ed.S, M.S., BCBA, is a behaviorist at the North Orange County Special Education Local Plan Area, where she is Autism Coordinator and supports five surrounding districts through research, professional development, and consultation for staff who work with individuals with autism. She is a Nationally Certified Behavior Analyst (BCBA), has a master of science degree in education, and has credentials in educational leadership, special education, and early childhood special education. She is also certified in behavior intervention case management, crisis intervention, and behavioral intervention for individuals with autism spectrum disorders. She has been involved with individuals with disabilities since the late 1990s and has worked as a teacher, coordinator, and university instructor. Christina coauthored *The Social Compass Curriculum* as a response to the tremendous need for social cognition support that has been apparent throughout her career. She has conducted several research projects and presented at conferences throughout Orange County.

Karen Chanin, M.S., P.P.S., is a school psychologist and behavior analyst. She currently supports the North Orange County Special Education Local Plan Area as its autism program specialist/school psychologist. Karen has more than 13 years of experience in working with children who have special needs. She holds a master of science degree in counseling: pupil personnel services, with advanced specialization in school psychology. Her experiences in working with children diagnosed with autism include providing in-home and at-school behavioral services, providing one-to-one support in the classroom, supervising staff working with children at home and at school, training teachers and other staff members on applied behavior analysis strategies, consulting with teachers, conducting assessments, and training others in autism-specific assessments.

ACKNOWLEDGMENTS

We would like to thank the North Orange County Special Education Local Plan Area, the Orange County Department of Education's S.U.C.S.E.S.S. (Systematic Utilization of Comprehension Strategies Ensuring Student Success) Project, and California State University at Fullerton for providing an environment of excellence. We would also like to thank our families, who allowed us the time to put together this book and its accompanying materials and who volunteered to be models for the photo supports (Race Chambers and Talia Chanin). Finally, we thank Nathan Smith for providing the illustrations, Jan Schrieber for creating the icons, and Ana Llorente for her prior graphic design work on the curriculum.

INTRODUCTION

Autism is a neurodevelopmental disorder that is typically identified or diagnosed at a young age, the symptoms of which can last a lifetime. It is a spectrum disorder, meaning individuals can present with the symptoms in many ways. There are several key characteristics of autism; however, social skills impairments are a core feature (American Psychiatric Association, 2000). Because social skills are the skills involved in interacting and communicating with others, the natural environment for teaching and practicing them is in a group setting. To best support learning, these skills should be taught within a group regularly and consistently, in a setting where a child is experiencing typical daily interactions and situations.

The Social Compass Curriculum is a research-based intervention package for teachers and school-based therapists to promote successful social interactions over the course of months and years. The curriculum is meant to be administered in a typical learning or social environment to all children who might benefit from the lessons but particularly to those with autism spectrum disorders (ASDs).

The curriculum includes 24 lessons divided among 4 different modules, represented by the 4 cardinal directions (north, east, south, west): Nonverbal Skills, Emotions, Social Problem Solving, and "We" Skills. Each lesson is taught using a five-step process that includes an explicit statement of the goal of the lesson, an explanation of the visual support for reinforcement throughout the lesson, a Social Compass story to provide a concrete example of the skill, an opportunity for students to model and rehearse the social skill from each lesson using the provided Self-Monitoring Data Sheet to ensure comprehension and record performance, and a Parent Follow-Up Page for generalization or ongoing practice and learning of the target social skills. (Printable, photocopiable versions of the Self-Monitoring Data Sheets and Parent Follow-Up Pages specific to each lesson are included in Appendix B and among the accompanying online materials.)

Even though the curriculum provides the same core material to all learners, it is highly individualized as the teacher's feedback is related to each individual student in each moment, and students are taught to practice and monitor their own understanding. For example, when the teacher delivers the core lesson content to an individual student about how to respond to another person who is holding up his or her hand, palm out, and facing the student, the feedback related to the social information is specific to that dyad in that moment. In this way, each occurrence or role play is a new and additional opportunity to learn the social skill. Progress across such role plays can be monitored using the student Self-Monitoring Data Sheet specific to each lesson.

The curriculum also takes into account that understanding the context of a gesture rather than focusing on a single gesture itself determines the ultimate meaning of a gesture.

For example, holding one's hand palm out in the direction of another person could mean different things. It might mean "wait" when a person who is talking with someone is approached by someone else, or it might mean "I need to catch my breath" when a person is hysterically laughing among a group of friends. Whole Body Listening must be considered (Trusdale, 1990; Wilson & Sautter 2011; Winner, 2000). Having the teacher provide feedback allows for contextually relevant cuing and prompting needed for each specific group within each lesson every time the skill is presented (Chamberlain, Kasari, & Rotheram-Fuller, 2007).

Visual supports in the form of drawings and icons are also used throughout the activities as reminders of key features of each social skill. Students and teachers may refer to these visual icons as reinforcement of skills learned. The icons used throughout this curriculum are provided on a single photocopiable handout in Appendix A and among the accompanying online materials, as well as on the poster that is included with this book.

WHAT YOU NEED TO KNOW ABOUT SOCIAL SKILLS IMPAIRMENTS IN AUTISM SPECTRUM DISORDERS

Social skills and abilities are evident—and important—from a very early age. At 4 months of age, typically developing children return a smile, share interests, share attention to activity with another person, and so forth. The Centers for Disease Control and Prevention (n.d.) described the social issues children with autism experience in the following manner:

> Social issues are one of the most common symptoms in all of the types of ASDs. People with an ASD do not have just social "difficulties" like shyness. The social issues they have cause serious problems in everyday life.
>
> Examples of social issues related to ASDs:
>
> - Does not respond to name by 12 months of age
> - Avoids eye-contact
> - Prefers to play alone
> - Does not share interests with others
> - Only interacts to achieve a desired goal
> - Has flat or inappropriate facial expressions
> - Does not understand personal space boundaries
> - Avoids or resists physical contact
> - Is not comforted by others during distress
> - Has trouble understanding other people's feelings or talking about own feelings

The CDC description goes on to explain,

> Some people with an ASD might not be interested in other people at all. Others might want friends, but not understand how to develop friendships. Many children with an ASD have a very hard time learning to take turns and share—much more so than other children. This can make other children not want to play with them.
>
> People with an ASD might have problems with showing or talking about their feelings. They might also have trouble understanding other people's feelings. (n.d.)

Unfortunately, some students with autism still lack even the most basic social skills that typically emerge very early in life well into high school and beyond. Can these skills be taught? They absolutely can, with specific targeted and intensive intervention to address these core impairments. The lessons selected for *The Social Compass Curriculum* are designed to develop and expand on these early skills, as they are based on evidence-based practices such as the use of applied behavior analysis interventions (e.g., cuing, prompting, modeling, providing feedback, teaching self-monitoring, systematically reinforcing a desired skill), visual and peer supports, and Social Stories. Social Stories as developed by Carol Gray (1994, 2010) are structured written and illustrated scenarios that provide the reader with the details of who, what, where, and when that apply to a targeted social behavior.

RESEARCH FOUNDATIONS OF *THE SOCIAL COMPASS CURRICULUM*

As social skills impairments are a core feature of autism, and because children spend much of their time in school, it is imperative that schools have effective and well-established programs on social skills for their students. Gresham, Sugai, and Horner (2001) concluded that effective social skills instruction needs to include teaching in natural settings such as at school, teaching in a group of peers for maintenance and generalization, and providing ongoing support to students through trained staff and peers. Much research has been conducted in the field of applied behavior analysis to identify the following components as essential in social skills instruction for children with ASDs (Krantz & McClannahan, 1998; Krasny, Williams, Provencal, & Ozonoff, 2003; McAffee, 2001; Weiss & Harris, 2001; White, Keonig, & Scahill, 2007; Wilczynski, Menousek, Hunter, & Mudgal, 2007):

- Making a skill concrete
- Modeling a skill
- Rehearsing or providing repetition of a skill
- Practicing through role-playing in highly structured environments
- Providing systematic reinforcement with feedback
- Planning for maintenance of new skills
- Generalizing specific skills in the natural environment

These applied behavior analysis "ingredients" are combined in *The Social Compass Curriculum* into a lesson format designed for educators to implement in classrooms. This curriculum offers a simple, classroom-ready, five-step approach to social skills instruction so that students experience increased opportunities for social success. By implementing and refining this curriculum in public schools with more than 300 students since 2003, with significant results in case studies, we found that social skills intervention can be delivered in schools at the intensity that is required to make socially significant change (Boyd & Ward, 2012).

Models of Research

In their 2003 article *Social Skills Interventions for the Autism Spectrum: Essential Ingredients and a Model Curriculum,* Krasny, Williams, Provencal, and Ozonoff recommended specific components that are essential for an effective social skills curriculum. This informative article inspired the inclusion of more specific visual supports and directives for how to use them in each lesson. In addition, each lesson in *The Social Compass Curriculum* is structured according to evidence-based components, which are discussed next. Ensuring that the targeted skill is observable and the teacher's language is comprehendible, for example, is addressed by providing a vignette of the skill. Further inspiration for *The Social Compass Curriculum* came from the seminal intervention known as Social Stories, developed by Carol Gray in 1991 (The Gray Center for Social Learning and Understanding, n.d.). Social Compass stories use icons and descriptive, easy-to-relate-to vignettes to provide valuable information about the social skill taught in each lesson.

Several activities are provided through rehearsal and role-playing steps to provide multiple opportunities for students to acquire the skill in a given lesson. Visual supports, illustrations, and icons are used to clarify the Social Compass story as well as support the understanding of the social skill concepts. The icons related to the skill concepts are representations of objects or tools that are dynamic and provide a mechanism to understand the ever-changing nature of social interactions rather than a static rule to follow. These visual supports are helpful for students and serve as quick reminders or prompts as skills are being learned in the classroom and in settings outside of school. Peers are involved so that activities are focused on others and contextually relevant (Chamberlain et al., 2007). Teacher and peer feedback on a student's role play of the skill is provided for reinforcement of a contextually relevant response, and a plan for generalization is provided in the form of worksheets for use at home and in the community. Worksheets are provided as a way to review and reinforce skills learned in each lesson, and they provide opportunities for students to monitor their understanding and progress on skills taught.

Education Initiatives

Federal legislation requires that students with disabilities be educated in the least restrictive environment (LRE); that is, with their peers, whenever possible (Individuals with Disabilities Education Improvement Act [IDEA] of 2004, PL 108-446). This mandate pushes for students with any range of disabilities to enjoy the many benefits of attending classes with their typically developing, same-age peers. To that end, this curriculum was developed to be used in a general education setting, with full participation by all students so that all students benefit.

Because of its reach to all students, *The Social Compass Curriculum* can be used in conjunction with the response to intervention (RTI) initiative used in schools throughout the United States. The RTI model recommends that standard behavioral expectations and academic instruction are presented first to all students (Tier 1). If certain students are not responsive to the larger group instruction, then targeted small-group interventions are applied (Tier 2), followed by intensive individualized programming (Tier 3) if necessary (Barnett, Daly, Jones, & Lentz, 2004; see Figure 1). To address behavioral expectations, social skills instruction is recommended for those who are in need of additional support, and as was discussed previously, the interactive and in-the-moment nature of social skills cannot be mastered in isolation. Ongoing small-group social skills intervention, such as that found in Tier 2 of the RTI model, may be necessary for some students, and *The Social Compass Curriculum* provides materials to that end.

HOW CAN *THE SOCIAL COMPASS CURRICULUM* HELP YOU?

This curriculum is designed to encourage healthy social-emotional development by teaching students critical social skills. It may be used by school staff during the course of a school day and year. Each lesson is broken into steps and can be delivered to a group in one 40-minute period or in four 10-minute sessions over different days. For example, Step 1 can be taught on Monday, Step 2 on Tuesday, Step 3 on Wednesday, and Step 4 on Thursday. Step 5 includes sending home the parent worksheet and can be reviewed with the class before sending it home on Friday. The entire curriculum is designed to be used across a school year and allows for flexibility in that the teacher can go back and review topics in which students are struggling. Visual supports, student worksheets, data sheets,

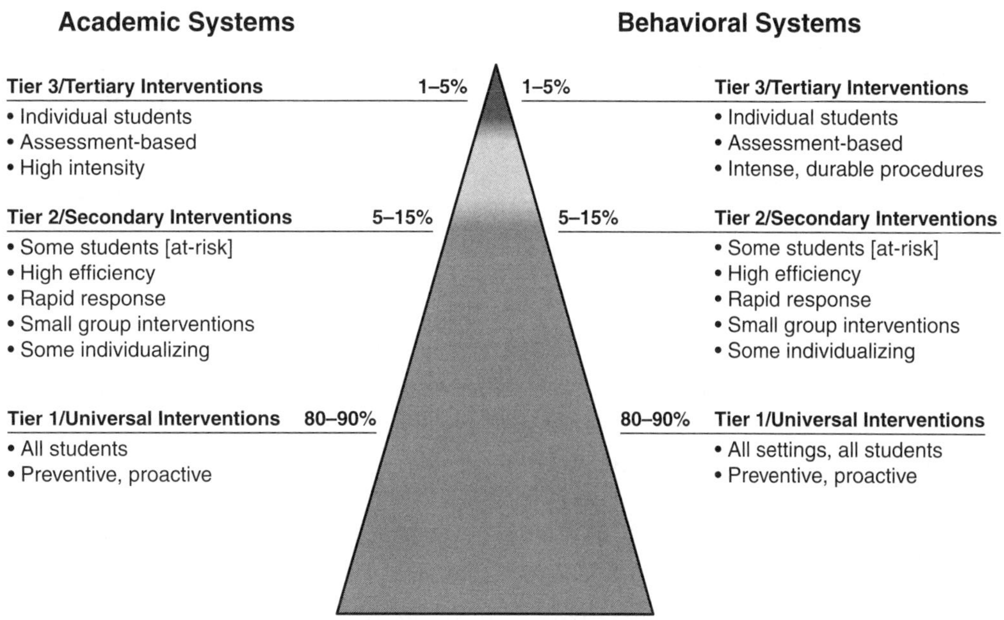

Figure 1. The three tiers of intervention. (From National Technical Assistance Center on Positive Behavioral Interventions and Supports. [2013]. *Academic and behavior triangle.* U.S. Department of Education, Office of Special Education Programs. University of Oregon; adapted by permission. www.pbis.org.)

and homework pages are included in each lesson and can be found in the appendixes and also among the accompanying online materials.

For those who choose to use *The Social Compass Curriculum* as part of a larger intervention plan, a more formal assessment is also recommended to establish a child's baseline performance and monitor progress and outcomes. Bellini's Autism Social Skills Profile (ASSP), for example, was developed to measure social functioning in individuals with ASDs and specifically to facilitate progress monitoring through an intervention process. The ASSP measures three domains—social reciprocity, social participation/avoidance, and detrimental social behaviors—and is available in the book *Building Social Relationships: A Systematic Approach to Teaching Social Interaction Skills to Children and Adolescents with Autism Spectrum Disorders and Other Social Difficulties* (Bellini, 2006).

USING THE CURRICULUM

As noted previously, *The Social Compass Curriculum* includes 24 lessons divided among the following 4 teaching modules: Nonverbal Skills, Emotions, Social Problem Solving, and "We" Skills. Each lesson contains step-by-step instructions to teach a skill through the use of a visual support, a story with reading comprehension questions, and a role-play and rehearse exercise, in addition to prompting and feedback through self-monitoring data recording and parent follow-up activities for generalization of the learned skills at home.

Step 1: Explain the Goal and Visual Support.

The goal states explicitly why the skill is important and how it will benefit the student personally. The teacher shows the visual support illustrating the skill to the student and explains it to help make the concept concrete. The visual supports provided in this curriculum aid the students in understanding that social skills are dynamic (Winner, 2000).

The visual supports in this curriculum represent interactive tools that can measure, label, adjust, and inform the user of the context and climate of social interactions. Hand-drawn illustrations of the visual supports appear in Step 1 of each lesson and complement the story illustrations. Graphics of visual icons or representations of the illustrations are also included and used for reinforcement on the students' Self-Monitoring Data Sheet and on the Parent Follow-Up Page for each lesson.

Step 2: Read the Social Compass Story.

The teacher reads a Social Compass story to the group to illustrate a specific skill within a relevant context. Each story describes a student with a problem who then resolves his or her issue with an explicit strategy. A set of reading comprehension questions is provided for immediate follow-up to ensure that the language of the story was meaningful (Franke & Durbin, 2011). One worksheet is provided per module (available in Appendix A and among the accompanying online materials); the correct answers for all lessons within that module appear on the worksheet, but only one answer is correct per lesson. In some cases, students may be able to argue that another answer works; as long as they can say how a previously learned strategy works for the current scenario, it is okay. It might make for a good class discussion to propose this alternate answer as also correct and to see how the group responds. As a curriculum, the stories in each lesson represent a sequence of skills that build on one another, allowing for review and use of previously learned visuals to be applied in the subsequent stories.

Step 3: Model and Rehearse.

Based on the best-practices research of applied behavior analysis (Krasny et al., 2003), the teacher models the skill and prompts students to demonstrate the isolated skill through labeling or imitating the modeled behavior (rehearse) as a group. The teacher reinforces correct behavior and invites honest and kind feedback for how other students can improve their behavior. The teacher mediates each dialogue as needed. The students record this data on the Self-Monitoring Data Sheet.

Step 4: Role-Play and Reinforce.

Students practice by demonstrating the skill within a structured social context, and the teacher and other students provide feedback on each student's performance. Students record their responses on the Self-Monitoring Data Sheet provided for each lesson. Most students are able to understand the 3-point rating system to rate their behavior on the worksheet. It is important that students track their own achievements during the use of *The Social Compass Curriculum,* as the progress of each student depends in part on his or her ability to accurately perceive his or her own performance. For students who cannot independently write short answers, a thumbs-up or thumbs-down gesture to evaluate performances is appropriate. These gestures also allow the teacher to monitor which students are engaged in the activity and how well they understand the task.

Step 5: Promote Generalization.

Each lesson concludes with a Parent Follow-Up Page that is sent home so that the students can continue to practice the skills at home and in the community. The icons used throughout the curriculum with each lesson also serve as visual supports or reminders and assist with generalization at home and beyond. As noted previously, all of the visual icons are on a handout and on a poster that can be hung in a classroom for quick and easy reminders for all students. Included as well are flashcards featuring one icon per card (with an explanation on the back) for those students requiring more targeted practice with a specific skill.

CONCLUSION

The Social Compass Curriculum includes lessons on a range of social situations and features stories and guidance for students about how to handle those situations. The curriculum is based on several research-based strategies and has been used and refined over 10 years. *The Social Compass Curriculum* contains stories, activities, and visual support that, in combination, help students learn skills to navigate the ever-changing "social climate."

The social climate is a metaphor for the ongoing mood of a group. There can be different social climates for each group. It is a teacher's job to prepare students for these different social climates and frequent changes in the social weather. By using *The Social Compass Curriculum,* teachers will equip their students with the following essential social skills: nonverbal skills, emotions, social problem solving, and "we" skills. Good luck, and enjoy the trip!

REFERENCES

American Psychiatric Association. (2000). *Diagnostic and statistical manual of mental disorders* (4th ed., text rev.). Washington, DC: Author.

Barnett, D.W., Daly, E.J., III, Jones, K.M., & Lentz, E., Jr. (2004). Response to intervention: Empirically based special service decisions from single case-designs of increasing and decreasing intensity. *Journal of Special Education, 38,* 66–80.

Bellini, S. (2006). *Building social relationships: A systematic approach to teaching social interaction skills to children and adolescents with autism spectrum disorders and other social difficulties.* Overland Park, KS: Autism Asperger Publishing.

Boyd, L., & Ward, D. (in press). Social Compass Curriculum: Case study analyses of social skills outcomes for students with autism. *SAGE Open.*

Centers for Disease Control and Prevention. (n.d.). *Autism spectrum disorders (ASDs).* Retrieved from http://www.cdc.gov/ncbddd/autism/signs.html

Chamberlain B., Kasari C., & Rotheram-Fuller, E. (2007). Involvement or isolation? The social networks of children with autism in regular classrooms. *Journal of Autism and Developmental Disorders, 37,* 230–242.

Franke, L., & Durbin, C. (2011). *Coaching comprehension, creating conversation: Nurturing narratives: Story-based language intervention for children with language impairments that are complicated by other developmental disabilities such as autism spectrum disorders.* Overland Park, KS: Autism Asperger Publishing.

Gray, C. (1994). *Comic strip conversations: Illustrated interactions that teach conversation skills to students with autism and related disorders.* Arlington, TX: Future Horizons.

Gray, C. (2010). *The new Social Story book: Over 150 Social Stories that teach everyday social skills to children with autism or Asperger's syndrome, and their peers* (10th ed., rev.). Arlington, TX: Future Horizons.

The Gray Center for Social Learning and Understanding. (n.d.). *Social Stories.* Retrieved from http://thegraycenter.org/social-stories

Gresham, F.M., Sugai, G., & Horner, R.H. (2001). Interpreting outcomes of social skills training for students with high-incidence disabilities. *Exceptional Children, 67,* 331–344.

Individuals with Disabilities Education Improvement Act (IDEA) of 2004, PL 108-446, 20 U.S.C. §§ 1400 *et seq.*

Krantz, P.J., & McClannahan, L.E. (1998). Social interactions skills for children with autism: A script for adding procedure for beginning readers. *Journal for Applied Behavioral Analysis, 31,* 191–202.

Krasny, L., Williams, B.J., Provencal, S., & Ozonoff, S. (2003). Social skills interventions for the autism spectrum: Essential ingredients and a model curriculum. *Child Adolescent Psychiatric Clinics of North America, 12*(1), 107–122.

McAffee, J. (2001). Using social stories and comic strip conversations to interpret social situations for an adolescent with Asperger syndrome. *Intervention in School and Clinic, 36*(5), 310–313.

National Technical Assistance Center on Positive Behavioral Interventions and Supports. (2013). *Academic and behavior triangle.* Retrieved from www.pbis.org

Weiss, M.J., & Harris, S.L., (2001). Teaching social skills to people with autism. *Behavior Modification, 25,* 785-802.

White, S.W., Keonig, K., & Scahill, L. (2007). Social skills development in children with autism spectrum disorders: A review of the intervention research. *Journal of Autism and Developmental Disorders, 37,* 1858-1868.

Wilczynski, S.M., Menousek, K., Hunter, M., & Mudgal, D. (2007). Individualized education programs for youth with autism spectrum disorders. *Psychology in the Schools, 44,* 653-666.

Winner, M.G. (2000). *Inside out: What makes a person with social cognitive deficit tick?* San Jose, CA: Think Social Publishing.

MODULE 1

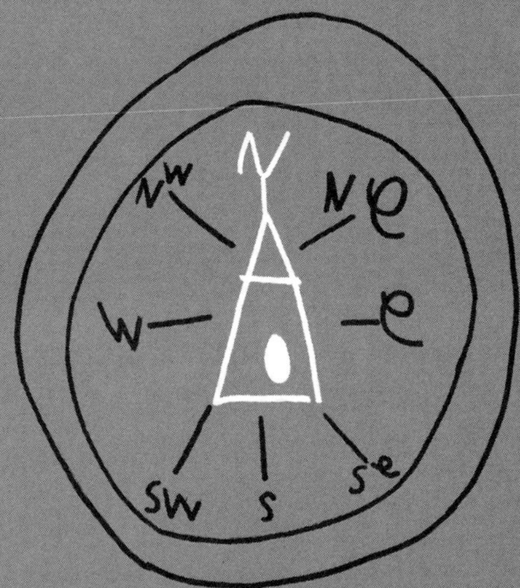

NONVERBAL SKILLS

Nonverbal skills involve individuals knowing how to read a social situation and use their bodies without using words to convey their intent. Nonverbal skills also involve reading other people's nonverbal behavior. *Nonverbal* refers to the actions and qualities of social behaviors. This module examines the nonverbal skills of body language, proximity, tone of voice, and social referencing. These behaviors are presented first in the curriculum because they are a part of every face-to-face interaction.

Understanding how to interpret these behaviors and respond accordingly is the focus of this module. The visual supports used to facilitate this understanding include Body Language Binoculars, a Proximity Compass, a Voice-o-Meter, and a Glance Gauge. Each lesson describes these tools in more detail.

Module 1 Lessons

LESSON 1A—BODY LANGUAGE/GESTURES

VISUAL SUPPORT: BODY LANGUAGE BINOCULARS

LESSON 1B—SPACE AND PROXIMITY

VISUAL SUPPORT: PROXIMITY COMPASS

LESSON 1C—VOLUME OF VOICE

VISUAL SUPPORT: VOICE-O-METER

LESSON 1D—SOCIAL REFERENCING

VISUAL SUPPORT: GLANCE GAUGE

LESSON 1A

BODY LANGUAGE/GESTURES

STEP 1. *EXPLAIN THE GOAL AND VISUAL SUPPORT.*

1a) Goal

Understanding what another person is communicating through the use of his or her body is imperative to understanding the correct message. In fact, some messages are only communicated through body language. Body language is communication that is conveyed without spoken words through the use of gestures and the position of the whole body in relation to others. We read body language to become aware of other people's intentions and know how to interpret their behavior. This skill will help students identify the social climate of the moment and respond appropriately.

1b) Visual Support

Binoculars allow one to see an image clearly from afar. This lesson uses Body Language Binoculars as an imaginary tool that prompts students to see another person's nonverbal communication by looking at his or her gestures and body position. This visual representation of binoculars reminds students to look at the whole scene to get a read on the full meaning of another's communication.

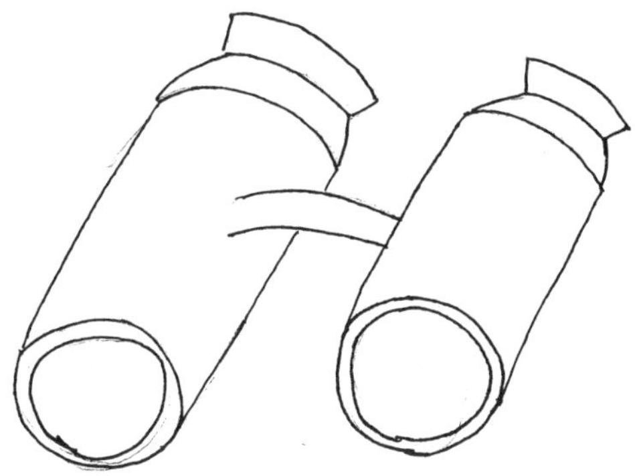

1c) Hand out Module 1, Lesson 1A
Self-Monitoring Data Sheets to the students.

Appendix A Appendix B

Provide all lesson handouts for the students to follow through with the remaining steps. (Note for all lessons: Waiting to give out these materials until this point is necessary only for students who are inclined to be distracted by the presence of the materials during the initial steps.)

STEP 2. *READ THE SOCIAL COMPASS STORY.*

2a) Read "Brad's Better Body Language."

Brad likes to talk. Usually, Brad likes to talk to everybody. One summer day at the mall, Brad felt tired. He just wanted to be by himself. After walking around in the mall for awhile, he went to the water fountain. Just then a girl came up to him and said, "Do you know where the bathroom is?" Without looking up from the fountain, he pointed to the left. He didn't feel like talking to anyone. But the girl asked again, "Excuse me, do you know where the bathroom is?" Again Brad just pointed without looking up at her. He said nothing but sighed loudly. He was frustrated with the girl for not understanding his body language. The girl began to cry. Brad looked up at her and now saw that she could not see him. She was blind. She had a cane. She could not see his body language.

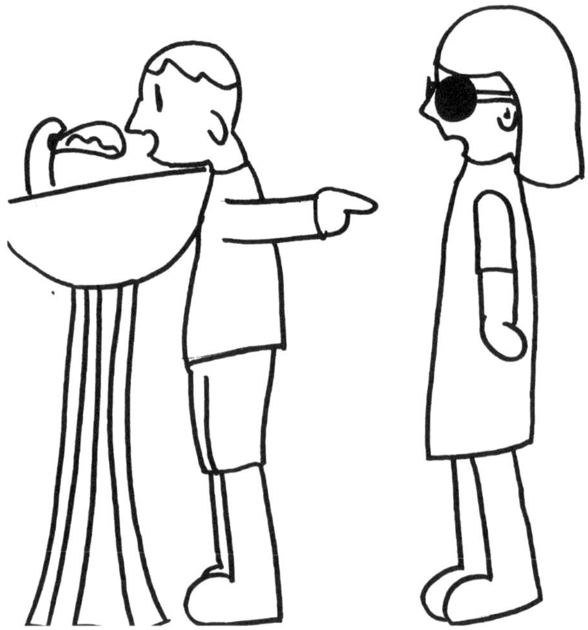

"Wow!" he thought. He was so surprised he took a moment to think about his Body Language Binoculars. He needed to use his binoculars to look at her body to decide how to respond. Because she couldn't see him point toward the bathroom, she did not understand his answer.

So next he said to her, "It is to your left, about 10 feet." She stopped crying, thanked him, and walked toward the bathroom. Brad felt good that he could help her. Now, he understood why she was still talking to him when he didn't feel like talking to her. He realized she couldn't see him to read his body language. If she could have seen him, she would have seen that he was busy. Brad was glad he had learned how to read body language. Someday, he hopes to find a way to help others learn it too.

2b) Have the students answer comprehension questions.

The answers should resemble the following:

MODULE 1 READING COMPREHENSION SHEET

1. What was the visual support? Select one.

X  ○  ○  ○ 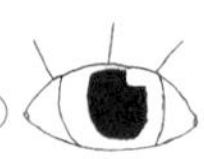

2. Who was the story about? Select one.

X Brad ○ Spencer ○ Victor ○ Steve

3. What was his problem? Select one.

X Not looking at speaker ○ Getting too close
○ Talking too loudly ○ Staring too long

4. What did he learn to do about it? Select one.
   - [x] Look at the speaker
   - [ ] Speak softly
   - [ ] Stand back
   - [ ] Stop staring

5. Draw or summarize the story.

   Brad didn't look and read the girl's body language the first time, but he learned to in the end.

STEP 3. *MODEL AND REHEARSE.*

1A HANDOUT GESTURE GUIDE

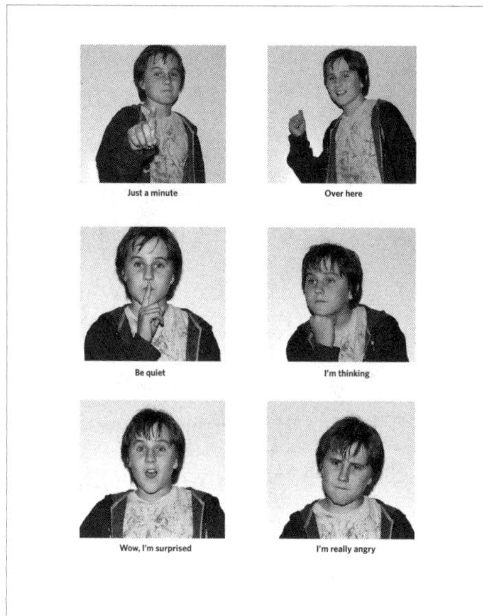

3a) Model the body language.

Model the body language from the Gesture Guide (found in Appendix B and among the accompanying online materials), and label it as you do it. Ask the group questions such as, "What do you think Brad's body language is telling you in this picture?" Let the students know that they can refer to the photos on the Self-Monitoring Data Sheet if they are unsure about what someone's body language is trying to convey to them. Have students mark on the Self-Monitoring Data Sheet for Line A.

3b) Have the students rehearse by imitating your model.

As the students imitate your model, have them record their performance on the Self-Monitoring Data Sheet for Line B.

In front of the small group, have one person model the gesture and the other person guess what gesture he or she is modeling.

1. The group should give a "thumbs up" if the guesser states the correct gesture or a "thumbs down" if the guesser is not correct. Note: If the student who is guessing is incorrect, prompt the student by providing some clues and allowing him or her another chance to respond.
2. Provide feedback on the student's performance of imitating gestures, and indicate how to complete this as a score on the Self-Monitoring Data Sheet.
3. Have the pair that is presenting the role play mark their individual score based on accuracy on Line C of their Self-Monitoring Data Sheets.
4. By the end of this activity, each student should have had the opportunity to model and guess at least one time before moving on to the role play.

   Check students' data sheets to ensure that they are scoring themselves accurately. Verbally reinforce students who score themselves accurately, and provide more instruction to those students who do not score themselves accurately.

3c) Prompt the students to mark their data for Line C on the Self-Monitoring Data Sheet.

I can role-play gestures from my Body Language Binoculars

○ by myself ○ with peer help ○ with teacher help

STEP 4. *ROLE-PLAY AND REINFORCE.*

4a) Have the students role-play responding to body language.

Have the students participate in additional role-play on how they would respond to the whole picture they see of someone exhibiting nonverbal behavior from their Body Language Binoculars.

1. Divide the students into groups of 2–4.
2. Each group should choose a gesture from the Gesture Guide to role-play.
3. Working as a team, the groups should create a scenario whereby one student imitates the gesture from the guide and the other students respond correctly to the gesture.

   For example, if one student is using his body language to ask others to be quiet, then the students could create a scenario in which they are all talking but once their peer uses his body language to show them that they should be quiet, they all become quiet.
4. The students who are observing the role play need to decide what gesture the group that is role-playing is using.
5. The role-play group should give the observing group a "thumbs up" or "thumbs down" depending on whether they are correct or not.
6. The students who are observing then decide whether they felt the role-play group reacted correctly or incorrectly to the nonverbal gesture.
7. Provide feedback.

4b) Prompt the students to mark their data on Line D of the Self-Monitoring Data Sheet.

I can respond to peers' nonverbal behavior in a role play

○ by myself ○ with peer help ○ with teacher help

STEP 5. *PROMOTE GENERALIZATION.*

Appendix B

Send home the Parent Follow-Up Page.

Follow-up directions are provided on the Parent Follow-Up Page.

LESSON 1B

SPACE AND PROXIMITY

STEP 1. *EXPLAIN THE GOAL AND VISUAL SUPPORT.*

1a) Goal

Individuals communicate their relation to others by how closely they stand to them. To ensure students are sending and receiving the correct message about their relationship with another, this lesson uses the Proximity Compass as a reminder.

1b) Visual Support

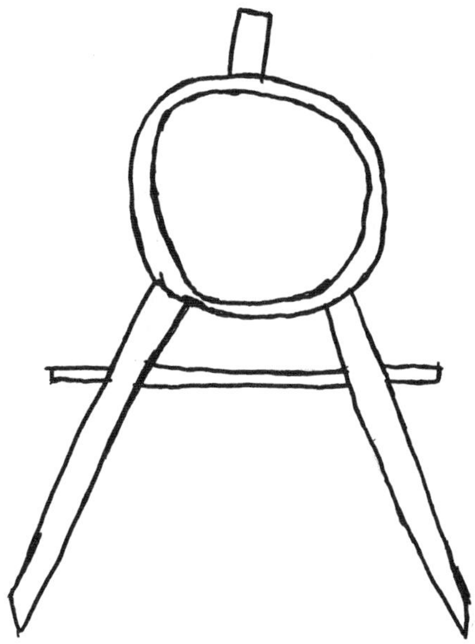

The Proximity Compass is a tool whereby students place themselves in the center and then draw circles around themselves to show their relationship with others. The distance between themselves and others is determined by their relationship with the other person. Close relations are represented by circles drawn close to the center point. This compass is a representation of a tool to determine the typical distance to stand in these given relationships. Examples of other people to include on the compass include family members, friends, acquaintances, and strangers.

1c) Hand out Module 1, Lesson 1B Self-Monitoring Data Sheets to the students.

Provide all lesson handouts for the students to follow through with the remaining steps.

STEP 2. *READ THE SOCIAL COMPASS STORY.*

2a) Read "Spencer's Space."

Spencer likes the park. Spencer likes to talk.

Spencer likes to talk to everybody, even everybody in the park. Sometimes Spencer talks to strangers. This isn't always a good idea because Spencer doesn't know what the strangers think or might do.

One day Spencer ran up to a baby in the park and started talking to the baby. He was standing very close to the baby in the stroller. His face was 2 inches away from the baby's face. The baby didn't know him. He was facing the baby and was in her space. The baby started to cry.

Something was wrong. Spencer asked himself, "What happened?" He remembered his Proximity Compass. He stopped and took a moment to think about his relationship to these people. They were strangers, which meant that they were in the furthest ring from him.

He said to the baby and mommy, "Oops, too close. I'm sorry."

Later he saw the baby and mommy again. He waved but he did not speak or get too close. He stayed 2 arms' lengths away. The baby and the mommy smiled. He smiled too. Spencer thought it was so nice to see a baby smile.

2b) Have the students answer comprehension questions.

The answers should resemble the following:

MODULE 1 READING COMPREHENSION SHEET

1. What was the visual support? Select one.

   ○    ☒    ○ 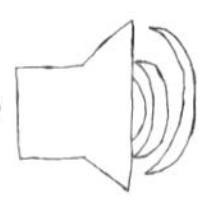   ○ 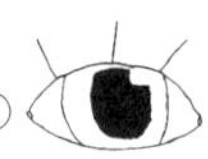

2. Who was the story about? Select one.

   ○ Brad   ☒ Spencer   ○ Victor   ○ Steve

3. What was his problem? Select one.

   ○ Not looking at speaker   ☒ Getting too close
   ○ Talking too loudly   ○ Staring too long

4. What did he learn to do about it? Select one.

   ○ Look at the speaker   ○ Speak softly
   ☒ Stand back   ○ Stop staring

5. Draw or summarize the story.

   Spencer got too close to the baby at first, but then he remembered the mother and baby were strangers and he should stay 2 arms' lengths away.

STEP 3. *MODEL AND REHEARSE.*

3a) Model appropriate proximity.

1. Use your body to demonstrate how close you would stand next to a family member (½ arm's length), a friend (½ arm's length to 1 arm's length), and acquaintance (1 arm's length), and a stranger (2 arms' lengths).

Appendix B

2. Direct the students to color in the ring on Line A on their Self-Monitoring Data Sheets as you model each social boundary. Supply Handout 1B (Appendix B) to students who need a reminder about what the rings represent.

1B HANDOUT
PROXIMITY COMPASS AND RELATIONSHIP RINGS

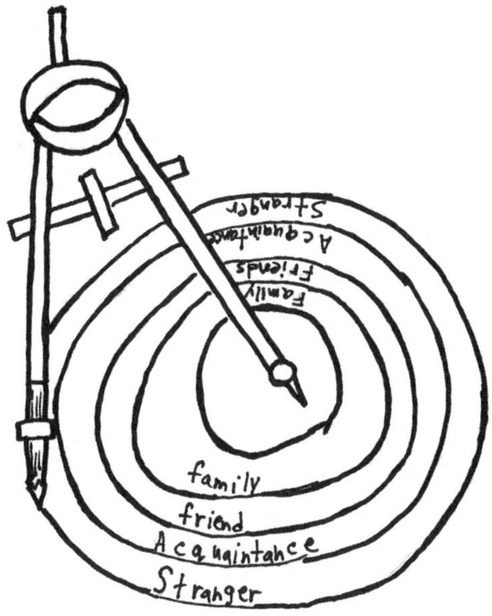

This lesson was inspired by *The Circles Curriculum*, published by James Stanfield Publishing (http://www.stanfield.com/products/family-life-relationships/circles-curriculum).

3b) Have the students rehearse standing in relation to others.

Have students stand up in pairs and practice where they stand in relationship to each other. Have one student be him- or herself while the other student pretends to be another person from the various categories discussed previously. Then have them switch.

3c) Prompt the students to mark their data on Line B of the Self-Monitoring Data Sheet.

I can imitate a model on where to stand in relation to another person given the type of relationship (or from choice of family, friend, acquaintance, stranger)

○ by myself ○ with peer help ○ with teacher help

STEP 4. *ROLE-PLAY AND REINFORCE.*

4a) Have the students do a large group role-play to demonstrate appropriate space and proximity.

Have the students all practice being in line for lunch.

1. All the students are to participate in this at the same time.
2. Tell the group to pretend they are lining up to buy lunch at school.
3. Allow them to get organized and demonstrate the appropriate proximity for a friend or acquaintance as they all stand in the lunch line.
4. Starting at one end of the line, ask each person to rejoin the line at the other end.
5. Have the others in the group give a "thumbs up" or "thumbs down" depending on whether they are displaying the appropriate proximity once they arrive back in line. Provide feedback on the students' performances, and indicate how to complete this as a score on the Self-Monitoring Data Sheet, Line C.

4b) Prompt the students to mark their data on the rest of the Self-Monitoring Data Sheet.

I can show appropriate distance with a partner in a role play of his or her choice

○ by myself ○ with peer help ○ with teacher help

STEP 5. *PROMOTE GENERALIZATION.*

Send home the Parent Follow-Up Page.

Follow-up directions are provided on the Parent Follow-Up Page.

LESSON 1C

VOLUME OF VOICE

STEP 1. *EXPLAIN THE GOAL AND VISUAL SUPPORT.*

1a) Goal

The goal is to have students practice how to recognize the volume and tone of their voices in order to use their voices effectively in activities and conversations. The way individuals use their voices communicates their intentions. People look for the words and the tone to gain meaning in another person's message.

1b) Visual Support

The Voice-o-Meter is a tool that rises and falls based on the volume of someone's voice, much like a thermometer rises and falls based on temperature. And, just as a thermometer conveys if something is too hot, too cold, or just right, the Voice-o-Meter can help students know if they are talking too loudly, too quietly, or just right for the environment they are in. For students who are ready for a challenge, tone levels can replace the emotions. Happy, mad, and sad can be substituted out for silly, serious, and sarcastic.

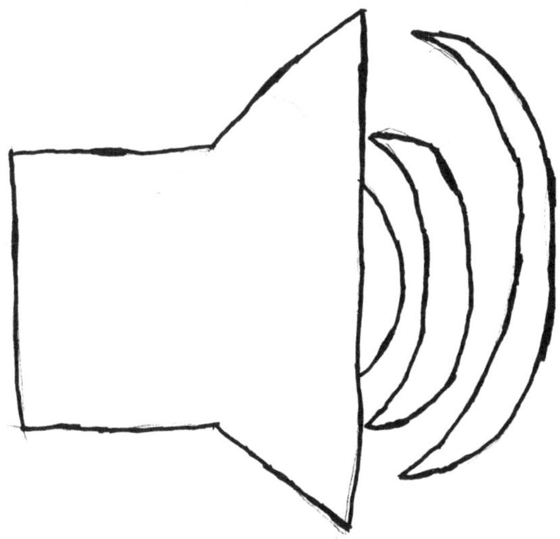

1c) Hand out Module 1, Lesson 1C Self-Monitoring Data Sheets to the students.

Provide all lesson handouts for the students to follow through with the remaining steps.

STEP 2. *READ THE SOCIAL COMPASS STORY.*

2a) Read "Victor's Loud Voice."

Victor likes school. Victor likes everybody in his sixth-grade class. One summer day he saw his fifth-grade teacher at the library.

Victor was so excited to see his teacher that he ran to him while screaming the teacher's name out loud from 10 feet away. Victor started telling his teacher in a loud voice all about his new school. He did not notice that his teacher was shrugging his shoulders, stepping away from him, squinting his eyes, and holding his ears with his hands.

Victor did not read the signs telling him that he was being too loud. Victor was still talking when his old teacher said, "It's nice to see you Victor, but I'm in a hurry, goodbye." Victor was sad that his teacher left and did not understand why he left in such a hurry. He checked his Voice-o-Meter in his head. Victor used a loud voice in an indoor place. He ran and screamed his teacher's name. His teacher looked surprised and in pain from the noise, then the teacher said goodbye.

The next time Victor saw his teacher, Victor gave him a little wave and a smile. He walked up to him and spoke softly. He watched his teacher's reaction. When his teacher looked relaxed, Victor felt relaxed too and continued to talk with his teacher. He finished his story about school, and his teacher told him a funny story. His teacher was impressed by Victor's change in behavior. Victor was proud too.

2b) Have the students answer comprehension questions.

The answers should resemble the following:

MODULE 1 READING COMPREHENSION SHEET

1. What was the visual support? Select one.

○  ○  ☒  ○ 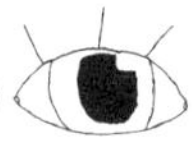

2. Who was the story about? Select one.

○ Brad ○ Spencer ☒ Victor ○ Steve

3. What was his problem? Select one.

○ Not looking at speaker ○ Getting too close
☒ Talking too loudly ○ Staring too long

4. What did he learn to do about it? Select one.

○ Look at the speaker ☒ Speak softly
○ Stand back ○ Stop staring

5. Draw or summarize the story.

Victor screams at his teacher, and his teacher gets annoyed and leaves. Victor remembers his Voice-o-Meter and uses his indoor voice.

STEP 3. *MODEL AND REHEARSE.*

3a) Model using appropriate volume of voice.

1. Show the Voice-o-Meter visual support. Explain to the students how to use the Voice-o-Meter.
2. Show them at what level their voice should be in various circumstances—for example, if they are inside, outside, in a noisy room, talking to someone, or in a quiet room while talking to someone.
3. Model the different volumes of your voice and have the students imitate the correct volume of your voice on their Voice-o-Meters and record that on Line A of their Self-Monitoring Data Sheets.
4. Provide students with feedback as to whether they imitated the volume of your voice correctly or incorrectly.
5. Next, add emotional tone to your voice (e.g., become louder or deeper when angry, quieter when shy, high pitched when silly).
6. For advanced students, have the students label the level of your emotional tone on the Voice-o-Meter on Line A of the Self-Monitoring Data Sheet.
7. Provide students with feedback.
8. Divide the students into pairs and have them label each other's voice levels.

3b) Prompt the students to mark their data on Line B of the Self-Monitoring Data Sheet.

I can identify my teacher's or partner's volume and tone

○ by myself ○ with peer help ○ with teacher help

STEP 4. *ROLE-PLAY AND REINFORCE.*

4a) Have the students role-play appropriate voice volumes.

1. Assign the students a volume on the Voice-o-Meter without revealing it to the group.
2. Have each student role-play the voice by standing in front of the group and talking at the voice level.
3. Have the students who are observing the role play indicate at what level their peer's voice is and whether he or she is using an indoor or outdoor voice. Also, have them label where and when it would be appropriate to use this voice level.
4. The student role-playing should give his or her peers feedback by giving them a "thumbs up" if they are correct or a "thumbs down" if they are incorrect. The teacher should also provide constructive feedback.
5. Change the level as everyone shows the ability to role-play, and add tone to the role play.

4b) Provide feedback.

Provide feedback on the students' performance for each role play. Indicate how to fill in each response on the Self-Monitoring Data Sheet.

4c) Prompt the students to mark their data on Line C of the Self-Monitoring Data Sheet.

I can role-play appropriate tone of voice with a partner for a situation of choice

○ by myself ○ with peer help ○ with teacher help

STEP 5. *PROMOTE GENERALIZATION.*

Appendix B

Send home the Parent Follow-Up Page.

Follow-up directions are provided on the Parent Follow-Up Page.

LESSON 1D

SOCIAL REFERENCING

STEP 1. *EXPLAIN THE GOAL AND VISUAL SUPPORT.*

1a) Goal

People use eye contact to gain information about their environment. Individuals look around themselves (glance) to gather information quickly, to communicate they are listening, or to try to be part of a group. People sometimes stare to convey intense emotions.

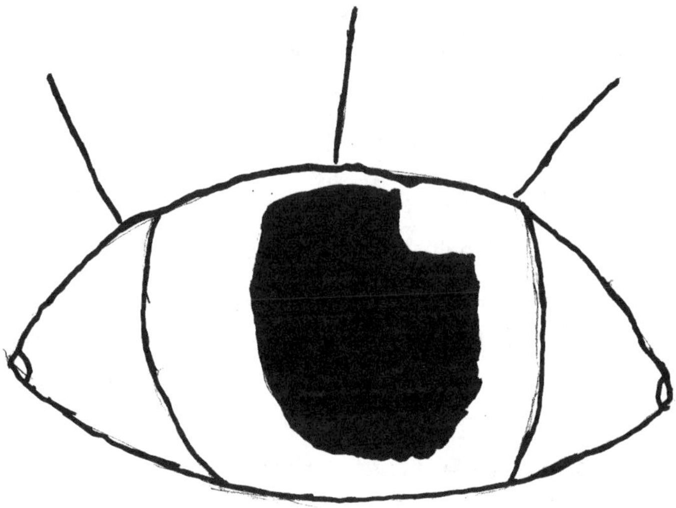

1b) Visual Support

The Glance Gauge is an imaginary tool similar to a timer. It represents the concept that the length of time a person looks at someone communicates information about one's intention. This tool reminds students how long to look around for quick information and how long to look to join in a group.

Appendix A Appendix B

1c) Hand out Module 1, Lesson 1D Self-Monitoring Data Sheets to the students.

Provide all lesson handouts for the students to follow through with the remaining steps.

STEP 2. *READ THE SOCIAL COMPASS STORY.*

2a) Read "Steve Used to Stare."

Steve likes to read and sometimes he likes to watch people. One day he watched a couple of classmates at the lunch table as they spoke to each other. Faye was talking to Laura and Allison. Faye was talking about funny things that her baby brother likes to do. Faye looked at Laura first and then at Allison as she told her story. Steve noticed that while Faye was talking, she looked back and forth between at Laura and Allison. Laura and Allison looked at each other and at Faye while she spoke. This was puzzling to Steve; he couldn't stop watching them. Steve was staring at the girls. He was fixed

on their eyes, he was watching constantly without turning his eyes away. The girls noticed he was staring at them. His staring made the girls very uncomfortable. They grimaced at him. Steve got embarrassed and looked away quickly. Without looking, he could hear them giggling. He knew they were making fun of him because he was looking at them for too long without communicating with them.

A moment later, he looked at them again. He saw that they had stopped paying attention to him and went on with their discussion. This was a relief to Steve. By looking away from them, Steve got them to stop paying attention to him. Then he remembered his Glance Gauge rules.

1. To check out the environment: Give a quick glance but do not stare.
2. To join a conversation: Look until the group invites you in.
3. Don't stare (unless you really are sure you want to express intense emotions).

The next day at lunch, Steve saw a few boys eating together. He looked at them and almost instantly they smiled when they saw him look. He smiled too and asked to join them, and they nodded yes. He was happy to be part of their group.

2b) Have the students answer comprehension questions.

The answers should resemble the following:

MODULE 1 READING COMPREHENSION SHEET

1. What was the visual support? Select one.

○  ○  ○  ☒ 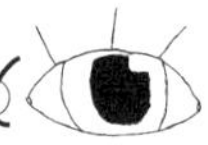

2. Who was the story about? Select one.

○ Brad ○ Spencer ○ Victor ☒ Steve

3. What was his problem? Select one.

○ Not looking at speaker ○ Getting too close
○ Talking too loudly ☒ Staring too long

4. What did he learn to do about it? Select one.
   ◯ Look at the speaker ◯ Speak softly
   ◯ Stand back ☒ Stop staring

5. Draw or summarize the story.
   Steve watched some girls to understand them better. They saw him staring and were not happy about it. He learned to only glance to gain information about others and to look longer when he wants to be part of the group.

STEP 3. *MODEL AND REHEARSE.*

3a) Model stare, glance, and look behaviors.

Refer students to their Glance Gauge. Model stare, glance, and look behaviors without labeling them yourself.

1. *Stare:* Show the students what staring looks like by staring for 10 seconds or more at someone in the group who has not invited the attention.
2. *Glance:* Show them social referencing for gaining information about a situation by glancing at a few people to see if they are paying attention. Verbalize out loud your observations and your behavior as you do this.
3. *Look:* Model using your eyes to indicate you want to join a group.
4. Instruct students to mark Line A on the Self-Monitoring Data Sheet regarding their accuracy in identifying the model's behavior.

3b) Have the students rehearse by playing a game.

1. Have the students rehearse looking skills by getting everybody in a circle to play "hot potato" (use any soft item to pass around the circle).
2. Explain to the students to toss the item to each other but to wait until someone is looking at them to know when it's okay to toss it.
3. Verbalize that glancing is not as strong a signal as maintained eye contact or staring.

3c) Prompt the students to mark their data on Line B on the Self-Monitoring Data Sheet.

There are 4 opportunities or trials for students to rate themselves.

I can look at my partner to know when to toss the bean bag based on referencing his or her body language

◯ by myself ◯ with peer help ◯ with teacher help

STEP 4. *ROLE-PLAY AND REINFORCE.*

4a) Have the students role-play social referencing.

1. Have the students stand in pairs in front of the class.
2. Have a third student approach the pair and use eye contact with each person to convey that he or she wants to enter the group.
3. Have a group member respond by inviting him or her into the group.
4. Observers can give a "thumbs up" when the nonverbal behavior conveys the interest to join the group. Add additional feedback.
5. Remind the students to complete Line C on their Self-Monitoring Data Sheets after each step. Again, there are 4 trials for repeated practice for each student.

4b) Prompt the students to mark their data on Line C of the Self-Monitoring Data Sheet.

I can role-play referencing a group to communicate the desire to join in from the outside of the circle

○ by myself ○ with peer help ○ with teacher help

STEP 5. *PROMOTE GENERALIZATION.*

Appendix B

Send home the Parent Follow-Up Page.

Follow-up directions are provided on the Parent Follow-Up Page.

MODULE 2

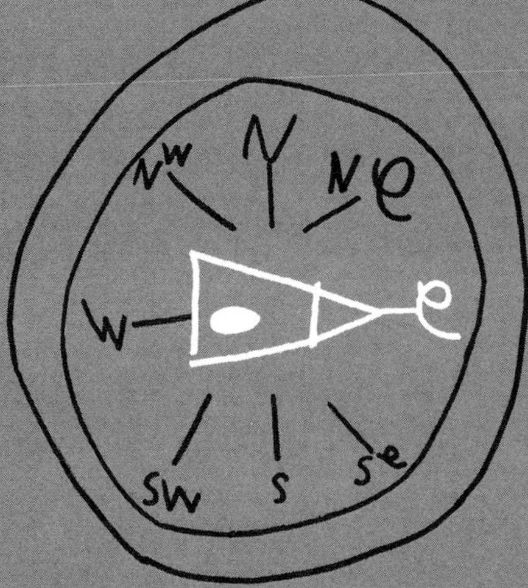

EMOTIONS

This module teaches concepts related to human emotions. For individuals to have a successful interaction with others, they must correctly identify their own and other people's emotional states, identify their emotional intensity and respond appropriately to others, and not be overly critical of themselves. Lessons in this module cover increasing emotional vocabulary and identifying others' feelings, recognizing the intensity of emotions, empathy, and positive self-talk.

For students to identify these emotional states in themselves and others, visual supports are provided for each lesson. These visual supports include an Emotional Climate Map, an Emotional Intensity Indicator, an Empathy Footprint, and a Positive Headset.

Module 2 Lessons

LESSON 2A—INCREASING EMOTIONAL VOCABULARY

VISUAL SUPPORT: EMOTIONAL CLIMATE MAP

LESSON 2B—IDENTIFYING INTENSITY OF FEELINGS

VISUAL SUPPORT: EMOTIONAL INTENSITY INDICATOR

LESSON 2C—EMPATHY

VISUAL SUPPORT: EMPATHY FOOTPRINT

LESSON 2D—POSITIVE SELF-TALK

VISUAL SUPPORT: POSITIVE HEADSET

LESSON 2A

INCREASING EMOTIONAL VOCABULARY

STEP 1. *EXPLAIN THE GOAL AND VISUAL SUPPORT.*

1a) Goal

Understanding others' emotions and contexts for emotions leads to better communication. This lesson helps students practice how to recognize emotional climates and use related vocabulary and in activities and conversations.

1b) Visual Support

A weather map indicates the current weather conditions in an area. Knowing the weather helps people prepare for being in that environment. This lesson uses the Emotional Climate Map to help students determine the mood or climate of the group. Learning how to navigate emotions in group situations is important to being comfortable and successful in a social situation.

1c) Hand out Module 2, Lesson 2A Self-Monitoring Data Sheets to the students.

Provide all lesson handouts for the students to follow through with the remaining steps.

STEP 2. *READ THE SOCIAL COMPASS STORY.*

2a) Read "Eddy Is Expanding His Emotional Vocabulary."

Eddy loves school. His favorite subjects are reading and spelling. He is a great speller and a good reader. He can read a word just once and remember how it is spelled. He loves new words or vocabulary. One thing he is not good at is reading a group situation. He didn't realize someone's face or eyes can give a lot of important clues to how someone is thinking or feeling.

This combination makes up an expression, or a look, that tells others how that person is *feeling*. What Eddy did not know was that there is a whole environment around one's

emotional behavior that provides information for a situation to make sense. It is called the emotional climate. He is excited to learn these new rules that remind him of a weather map. Then he can expand his ever-growing vocabulary to include an emotional climates. He can learn new words that tell about a group of people's emotions in specific conditions. Some emotional climate words include

Sunny/Breezy: A carefree, happy situation where one can do what he or she wants to do and can talk freely.

Heavy precipitation/showers: This is when the weather or the situation is requiring one to pay attention to watch what is coming at him or her—such as rain, snow, sleet, or wind—and to prepare accordingly.

Foggy: This condition describes an unclear atmosphere, when one isn't sure what events lie ahead. One should proceed with caution and remain alert.

Eddy knows that printed words are easy for him to read and remember. Reading faces is a bigger challenge for him. He is going to practice looking at people's faces and reading faces more.

2b) Have the students answer comprehension questions.
The answers should resemble the following:

MODULE 2 READING COMPREHENSION SHEET

1. What was the visual support? Select one.

☒  ○ 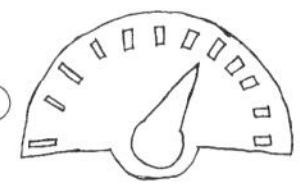 ○ 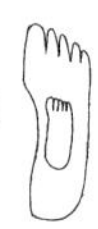 ○ 

2. Who was the story about? Select one.

☒ Eddy ○ Ida ○ Emanuel ○ Cory

3. What was his or her problem? Select one.

○ Not managing intense feelings
○ Doesn't know how to show he or she cares about others
○ Being mean to oneself
☒ Can't read faces to tell how people are feeling

4. What did he or she learn to do about it? Select one.
   ☒ Read emotions ○ Be nice to oneself
   ○ Talk about intense feelings ○ Help make people feel better

5. Draw or summarize the story.
   Eddy couldn't read faces to know how someone is feeling. He learned to read people's faces.

STEP 3. *MODEL AND REHEARSE.*

3a) Model the emotion for each climate and have students label the emotion.

Model various emotions (e.g., cheerful and carefree, serious and on task, highly attentive and on alert) Before you begin, explain that weather dictates how we behave. The emotional climate also dictates how we behave. List these conditions as "emotional climates," then model the corresponding behaviors:

1. Sunny: cheerful, carefree interaction
2. Rainy: serious and focused
3. Thunderbolt: high-alert state, pay attention to what is next

Have the students label on Line A of the Self-Monitoring Data Sheet the behavior you displayed for each emotional climate. Remind students that they may use the map as a reference.

3b) Have the students rehearse by imitating your model.

Ask the students to imitate the expected behavior for each emotional climate provided.

3c) Prompt the students to mark their data for Line B on the Self-Monitoring Data Sheet.

I can imitate emotional states during a role play

○ by myself ○ with peer help ○ with teacher help

STEP 4. *ROLE-PLAY AND REINFORCE.*

4a) Have the students role-play as a group, responding to your instructions to pretend they are in the following emotional climates.

—At the library during silent reading time
—In a park with several other students playing
—In the classroom when receiving instructions

1. Divide the students into groups of 2–4.
2. Each group should choose a climate to role-play his or her own scenario.

3. Working as a team, the groups should create a scenario whereby one student imitates the gesture from the guide and the other students respond correctly to the gesture.

   For example, if one student is using his body language to ask others to be quiet, then the students could create a scenario in which they are all talking but once the peer uses his or her body language to show them that they should be quiet, they all become quiet.

4. The students who are observing the role play need to decide what gesture the group that is role-playing is using.
5. The role-play group should give the observing group a "thumbs up" or "thumbs down" depending on whether they are correct or not.
6. The students who are observing then decide whether they felt the role-play group reacted correctly or incorrectly to the nonverbal gesture.
7. Provide feedback.

4b) Prompt the students to mark their data on Line C of the Self-Monitoring Data Sheet.

I can respond to others' emotional states in a role play

○ by myself ○ with peer help ○ with teacher help

STEP 5. *PROMOTE GENERALIZATION.*

Appendix B

Send home the Parent Follow-Up Page.

Follow-up directions are provided on the Parent Follow-Up Page.

LESSON 2B
IDENTIFYING INTENSITY OF FEELINGS

STEP 1. *EXPLAIN THE GOAL AND VISUAL SUPPORT.*

1a) Goal

The goal of this lesson is for students to correctly identify intense feelings in themselves and to express those intense feelings in an appropriate and safe manner to avoid creating conflict.

1b) Visual Support

Like a barometer that reads the air pressure in an environment, this lesson uses an Emotional Intensity Indicator to gauge the degree to which an emotion is demonstrated. Social situations require individuals to match their emotional intensity to a given situation. The image of a gauge that measures intensity reminds students to take a reading of their own intensity for any given situation.

Appendix A Appendix B

1c) Hand out Module 2, Lesson 2B Self-Monitoring Data Sheets to the students.

At this time, also provide all lesson handouts for the students to follow through with the remaining steps.

STEP 2. *READ THE SOCIAL COMPASS STORY.*

2a) Read "Ida's Story of Intense Feelings."

At school, many people have conversations. Some conversations are between classmates who are friends. Some conversations are friendly and some are not. Sometimes someone's feelings get hurt.

Ida had a conversation with a girl that ended badly. Ida asked the girl to go to a movie with her, and the girl laughed at her. The girl didn't know how much this hurt Ida's feelings. Ida was mad. She was so mad that when she saw the girl later that day, she pushed her. Now the girl was afraid of her. Ida's behavior scared the girl, and the girl didn't want to see her again. Ida was sent to the principal's office. The principal explained to Ida that she needed to let the pressure out before she got so intense that she screamed or pushed.

Then, Ida imagined her Emotional Intensity Indicator, measuring the pressure she felt inside when her feelings got hurt. She thought when the pressure gauge registered "high pressure" that she had to find an appropriate way to relieve it. She realized that screaming (and pushing) were dangerous behaviors. She wanted to make and keep friends.

Ida learned to let out the pressure of intense feelings by venting, or expressing her "high pressure" emotions to a trusted friend. Venting is to let out the "hot air" or the intense emotions in a controlled way. Ida can control her intense feelings by walking away and talking it out with another person. This is a good option for everyone.

2b) Have the students answer comprehension questions.

The answers should resemble the following:

MODULE 2 READING COMPREHENSION SHEET

1. What was the visual support? Select one.

○  ☒ 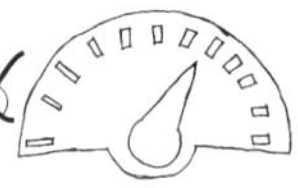 ○  ○ 

2. Who was the story about? Select one.

○ Eddy ☒ Ida ○ Emanuel ○ Cory

3. What was his or her problem? Select one.

☒ Not managing intense feelings
○ Doesn't know how to show he or she cares about others
○ Being mean to oneself
○ Can't read faces to tell how people are feeling

4. What did he or she learn to do about it? Select one.

○ Read emotions ○ Be nice to oneself
☒ Talk about intense feelings ○ Help make people feel better

5. Draw or summarize the story.

Ida wanted to spend time with a girl, but the girl just laughed at her. Ida got really mad and pushed the girl. Ida was sent to the principal's office, and the principal told her that she needed to learn to show her intense feelings in another way. Ida learned how to vent so that the next time she got angry people weren't scared of her.

STEP 3. *MODEL AND REHEARSE.*

3a) Model emotional intensity.

Model each of the emotions on the Emotional Intensity Indicator (found in Appendix B and among the accompanying online materials). Ask students to label each emotion out loud as you perform it. Direct students to record their responses on Line A of the Self-Mentoring Data Sheet.

2B HANDOUT
EMOTIONAL INTENSITY INDICATOR

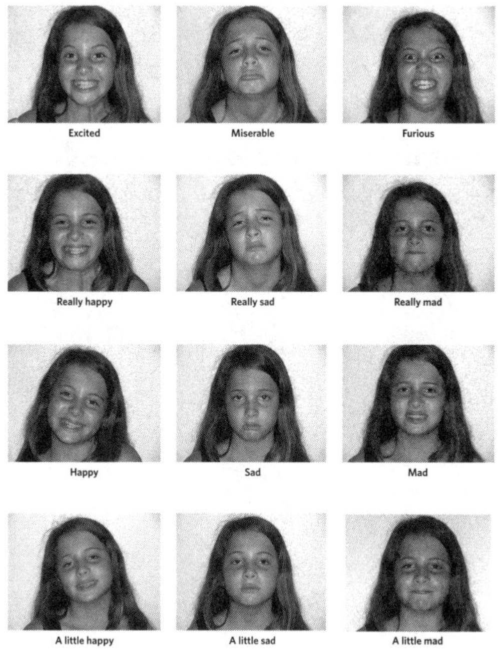

3b) Have the students rehearse by imitating emotions.

Have the students rehearse by imitating the emotions on the Emotional Intensity Indicator handout (found in Appendix B and online) as you call out the emotion or point to its picture. Prompt the students to mark their data for Line B on the Self-Monitoring Data Sheet.

I imitate feelings from the Emotional Intensity Indicator

○ by myself ○ with peer help ○ with teacher help

STEP 4. *ROLE-PLAY AND REINFORCE.*

4a) Have the students role-play identifying the intensity of feelings.

In groups of at least three, have the students role-play reacting calmly to an intense situation by walking away and venting. Example situations include the following:

—Getting an answer wrong in class
—Having your parents tell you to eat something you don't like
—Seeing someone break the rules of a game
—Having people laugh at you
—Having to quit working on something you wanted to finish
—Doing things incorrectly/making mistakes

4b) Prompt students to record each personal response on Line C of the Self-Monitoring Data Sheet.

I can role-play intense feelings and walk away

○ by myself ○ with peer help ○ with teacher help

Provide feedback through verbal reinforcement when the student's response is correct. Provide corrections with explanations when the student's response is incorrect. Have the student's peers provide feedback to others by providing him or her with a "thumbs up" or "thumbs down" during each activity.

STEP 5. *PROMOTE GENERALIZATION.*

Send home the Parent Follow-Up Page.

Follow-up directions are provided on the Parent Follow-Up Page.

LESSON 2C

EMPATHY

STEP 1. *EXPLAIN THE GOAL AND VISUAL SUPPORT.*

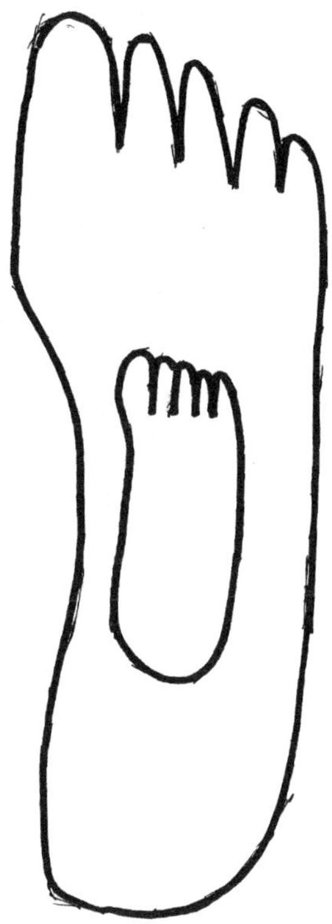

1a) Goal

Being a friend requires people to show empathy. The goal of this lesson is to help students understand and recognize empathy and practice expressing empathetic behavior toward others.

1b) Visual support

The visual support for this lesson is the Empathy Footprint. The image illustrates the concept of putting oneself in someone else's shoes so students can imagine how it would feel if they were in someone else's situation. The hole that is left behind from a footprint is the space students imagine filling to understand another person's perspective.

1c. Hand out Module 2, Lesson 2C Self-Monitoring Data Sheets to the students.

Provide all lesson handouts for the students to follow through with the remaining steps.

STEP 2. *READ THE SOCIAL COMPASS STORY.*

2a) Read "Emanuel Shows Some Empathy."

Emanuel is a great speller. Emanuel can spell *E M P A T H Y,* but he doesn't know what it means. He can pronounce it, "em-path-eee," but he still doesn't know what it means. Because Emanuel doesn't know what *empathy* means, he decided to ask his teacher.

His teacher explained that empathy is being able to identify with another person's circumstances and emotions. But he still doesn't really know what that feels like or how to show it (or so he thinks). To feel empathy means that Emanuel understands that other people experience situations, feelings, or motives differently than he does but that he can think about their experiences too even if he isn't feeling it firsthand. Sometimes these situations and feelings are similar to his.

Emanuel showed empathy just the other day. He was on the playground after lunch. His class was picking teams for a basketball game. The kids were excited to play. After most of the kids were already picked, he saw that his friend, Steve, did not get picked on a team. He remembered how he felt when that happened to him. Next Emanuel watched Steve make a face: Steve frowned, his eyes got wet and red, and his mouth turned down. Emanuel knew this facial expression. He knew that Steve was feeling sad. Then Steve ran away from the kids and the basketball court, slumped down behind a tree, and began to cry.

By seeing this whole situation, Emanuel knew Steve's reason for feeling this way and for running away. Emanuel had been in that same situation before. He remembered being hurt. Then he imagined the Empathy Footprint. He imagined putting his feet in Steve's shoes right now as if he were Steve. Emanuel imagined that Steve felt the team thought Steve was a bad player. So, he thought about what he could say to show Steve that he understood Steve's emotions. Emanuel followed his friend to the tree. Emanuel wanted to show Steve the he understood how Steve was feeling right then and did so by saying, "We always save the best for last. Come be on our team." They both laughed. Emmanuel knew just how Steve felt, and telling Steve this made him feel so much better.

2b) Have the students answer comprehension questions.
The answers should resemble the following:

MODULE 2 READING COMPREHENSION SHEET

1. What was the visual support? Select one.

○  ○ 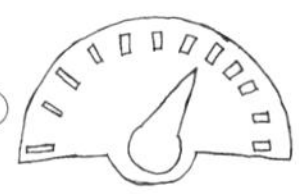 ☒  ○ 

2. Who was the story about? Select one.

○ Eddy ○ Ida ☒ Emanuel ○ Cory

3. What was his or her problem? Select one.

○ Not managing intense feelings
☒ Doesn't know how to show he or she cares about others
○ Being mean to oneself
○ Can't read faces to tell how people are feeling

4. What did he or she learn to do about it? Select one.

○ Read emotions ○ Be nice to oneself

○ Talk about intense feelings ☒ Help make people feel better

5. Draw or summarize the story.

Emanuel learned to understand why Steve was sad and went to him. He used kind words that made Steve feel better.

STEP 3. *MODEL AND REHEARSE.*

3a) Model empathy.

Read to the students the following three scenarios. Have the students identify the empathetic statements in each story. Assist them with identifying the empathic phrases (bolded for the teacher) by modeling empathy when saying the correct phrase. Ask students to circle the correct statements for each story on Line A of the Self-Monitoring Data Sheet.

1. Jonny is playing soccer at school after lunch. He kicks the ball to Bob. Bob kicks the ball to Jonny and it hits Jonny in the face. Jonny covers his face with his hands and falls to the ground. Bob runs over to him and says, **"I am so sorry, are you okay?"** Jonny says "Yes, I will be alright in a minute."
2. The whole class is outside as school is dismissed. The students form a conga line, and everyone joins in but Chris. A girl says to Chris, **"Join in."** As he approaches the line, a student rushing past him bumps into him with his backpack, keeps running by, and says, "Sorry, it was an accident."
3. During a basketball game, Alex bumped into Brandon and Brandon fell down. Brandon shouts at Alex, "Hey, cut it out!" Alex says, "It was an accident!" Brandon tells his coach, and his coach says, **"I'm sorry that happened to you; are you okay?"**

3b) Have students rehearse empathy by imitating your model.

Have the students imitate teacher-modeled empathetic statements. Prompt the students to mark their data for Line B of the Self-Monitoring Data Sheet.

I can imitate empathetic statements

○ by myself ○ with peer help ○ with teacher help

STEP 4. *ROLE-PLAY AND REINFORCE.*

4a) Have the students role-play recognizing empathy.

1. Have the students break into three groups and role-play the three scenarios you read to them previously (or create their own, if they are advanced).
2. Observe students providing feedback for each role play. Identify the presence or absence of an empathetic statement by giving "thumbs up" or "thumbs down."
3. Provide feedback to the students based on their performances and their feedback during the session.

4b) Prompt the students to mark their data on Line C of the Self-Monitoring Data Sheet.

I can role-play empathy for others in a situation of choice

○ by myself ○ with peer help ○ with teacher help

STEP 5. *PROMOTE GENERALIZATION.*

Appendix B

Send home the Parent Follow-Up Page.

Follow-up directions are provided on the Parent Follow-Up Page.

LESSON 2D

POSITIVE SELF-TALK

STEP 1. *EXPLAIN THE GOAL AND VISUAL SUPPORT.*

1a) Goal

The goal of this lesson is for students to practice how to recognize the messages they send themselves and to use positive self-talk in activities and conversations.

1b) Visual Support

Earphones carry an auditory message to a user's ears. The visual support for this lesson is a Positive Headset, which is an imaginary tool that sends only positive messages to the user. The Positive Headset reminds students to have a positive mind-set. Students can use this image as a visual reminder that positive self-talk feeds positive information into their minds.

1c) Hand out Module 2, Lesson 2D Self-Monitoring Data Sheets to the students.

Provide all lesson handouts for the students to follow through with the remaining steps.

STEP 2. *READ THE SOCIAL COMPASS STORY.*

2a) Read "Critical Cory."

Cory is very smart. Cory is good at math. Cory is almost always the first to know the answer in class. But sometimes Cory makes a mistake. Cory starts to cry when he gives the wrong answer. Cory's teacher explains to him that he is being too critical. It is okay to be wrong some of the time. Nobody is perfect. Cory is being mean to himself by getting so upset over a little mistake. He is very smart, but he is not perfect. Cory feels he has to be perfect to be smart. His teacher explains that smart people make mistakes just like anybody else. But smart people learn from their mistakes. They learn the right answers and learn to respect themselves as just "being human." Being human means they aren't supposed to be perfect.

When Cory makes a mistake, instead of crying, he remembers to put on his Positive Headset so that he can say to himself, "Better luck next time!" This makes Cory feel so much better than crying. Cory knows life can be hard. And because he is not perfect, he will make mistakes. And mistakes are okay. Being mean to yourself or others is not okay. Cory remembers to tell his friends when they mess up: "Better luck next time." This makes everyone happy.

2b) Have the students answer comprehension questions. The answers should resemble the following:

MODULE 2 READING COMPREHENSION SHEET

1. What was the visual support? Select one.

○  ○ 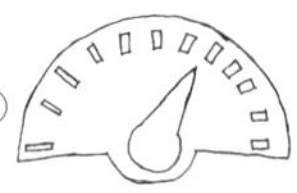 ○  ☒ 

2. Who was the story about? Select one.

○ Eddy ○ Ida ○ Emanuel ☒ Cory

3. What was his or her problem? Select one.

○ Not managing intense feelings
○ Doesn't know how to show he or she cares about others
☒ Being mean to oneself
○ Can't read faces to tell how people are feeling

4. What did he or she learn to do about it? Select one.

○ Read emotions ☒ Be nice to oneself
○ Talk about intense feelings ○ Help make people feel better

5. Draw or summarize the story.

Cory used to get upset when he got math problems wrong. His teacher taught him that smart people make mistakes. He learned to be nicer to himself.

STEP 3. *MODEL AND REHEARSE.*

3a) Model positive self-talk.

Tell the students that you will say some self-talk statements out loud. Tell them to listen for which is an example of positive self-talk. Emphasize the positive statement (bolded for the teacher's reference) appropriately to model it. Ask the students to circle the example of positive self-talk on Line A of the Self-Monitoring Data Sheet.

—I am terrible at this!
—I am always last!
—I will do it better next time!
—I will never give up!

3b) Have students rehearse by labeling your model.

Act out for the students situations with a negative implication but in which you remember to be nice to yourself. For example, model positive self-talk when getting a math problem wrong and saying something such as, "Oops, I made a mistake. That's okay; I'll try again." Give four examples—some positive and some negative. The students will put a check mark on the Self-Monitoring Data Sheet for each positive example trial.

3c) Prompt the students to mark their data for Line B on the Self-Monitoring Data Sheet.

I can label positive self-talk in written statements

○ by myself ○ with peer help ○ with teacher help

STEP 4. *ROLE-PLAY AND REINFORCE.*

4a) Have the students role-play positive self-talk.

1. Place the students in pairs.
2. Give each pair a new challenging situation to act out (e.g., losing a turn while playing a board game, getting tagged out in a sport, making a mistake on schoolwork, getting an answer wrong when called on in class). Ask each pair to role-play by saying out loud a potential positive self-talk statement.
3. Have the class provide additional examples of positive self-talk to the group.
4. Provide each student with reinforcement for correct performances. Highlight for the class examples of positive self-talk statements that were used. Have peers and students provide feedback and reinforcement during each activity.

4b) Prompt the students to mark their data on Line C of the Self-Monitoring Data Sheet.

I can use positive self-talk in role plays

○ by myself ○ with peer help ○ with teacher help

STEP 5. *PROMOTE GENERALIZATION.*

Appendix B

Send home the Parent Follow-Up Page.

Follow-up directions are provided on the Parent Follow-Up Page.

MODULE 3

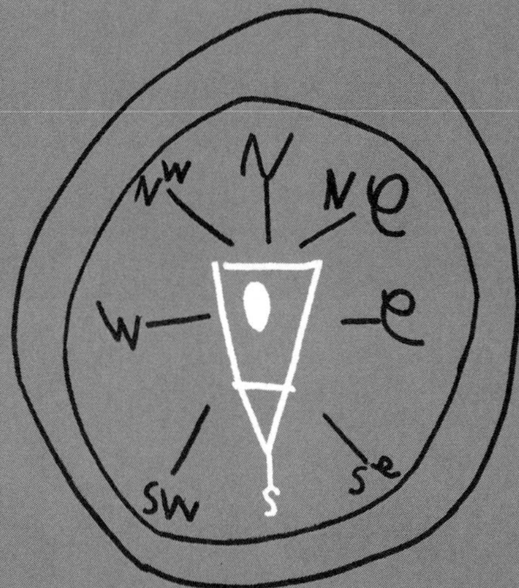

SOCIAL PROBLEM SOLVING

Social problem-solving skills help individuals interact successfully with others. Learning these skills may help students experience more positive social adjustment, deal better with stress, and improve their social behavior. In this module, students will practice remaining on topic during conversations, remaining focused whether in class or out of class, handling changes in routines, resisting tattling, handling teasing, controlling anger, and avoiding being left out of a group.

The focus of this model is for students to learn how to manage the multiple social situations that can come up in a group, in the classroom, or at school. Building on this goal, portions of the Module 3 reading comprehension sections require students to give narrative answers to social problem-solving questions. The visual supports for this module include a Relevance Radar, a Trail Marker, a GPS (Group Problem Solver) Alert, a Self-Portrait, a Handle, a Self-Controller, and a Membership Card.

Module 3 Lessons

LESSON 3A—STAYING ON TOPIC

VISUAL SUPPORT: RELEVANCE RADAR

LESSON 3B—PAYING ATTENTION

VISUAL SUPPORT: TRAIL MARKER

LESSON 3C—ACCEPTING CHANGE IN ROUTINES

VISUAL SUPPORT: GPS ALERT

LESSON 3D—RESISTING TATTLING

VISUAL SUPPORT: SELF-PORTRAIT

LESSON 3E—HANDLING TEASING

VISUAL SUPPORT: HANDLE

LESSON 3F—USING SELF-CONTROL

VISUAL SUPPORT: SELF-CONTROLLER

LESSON 3G—AVOIDING BEING LEFT OUT

VISUAL SUPPORT: MEMBERSHIP CARD

LESSON 3A

STAYING ON TOPIC

STEP 1. *EXPLAIN THE GOAL AND VISUAL SUPPORT.*

1a) Goal

The goal of this lesson is to teach students to pay attention to the topic of conversation and participate appropriately. Sometimes students want to share something unrelated to a lesson or conversation, so this lesson will illustrate how to stay on topic and avoid "blurting" behavior.

1b) Visual Support

The Relevance Radar tool is a visual reminder for students to stay on topic during verbal interactions. It detects when relevant information is in range and helps students avoid sharing inappropriate information at the wrong time.

1c) Hand out Module 3, Lesson 3A Self-Monitoring Data Sheets to the students.

Provide all lesson handouts for the students to follow through with the remaining steps.

STEP 2. *READ THE SOCIAL COMPASS STORY.*

2a) Read "Blurting Bob."

Bob is a smart student. He goes to school with other smart kids. One way he shows he is smart is by asking questions or making statements about the world. When Bob makes a statement that is off the topic that is being discussed in that moment, his teacher becomes frustrated with him. Bob doesn't understand why his teacher gets frustrated. His teacher feels frustrated because it is difficult to teach all of the students if she is interrupted by comments that have nothing to do with what they are learning.

The teacher thinks that Bob is smart, but she does not understand why he isn't thinking about her feelings or the other students' feelings when he calls out in class. Blurting slows down the teacher. This is not fair for others. Bob is just trying to have a conversation with the teacher by himself. But he is part of the group. He has to stay on topic.

He has to think about what the topic is. What is on target or relevant to the conversation? He remembers his Relevance Radar. He imagines himself holding the radar, and the radar blips when he is on topic. If he is talking about something that is not part of the discussion, his radar is silent. If what he wants to say is not on the radar or not related to the discussion, then he should not say it. This is a way to be polite.

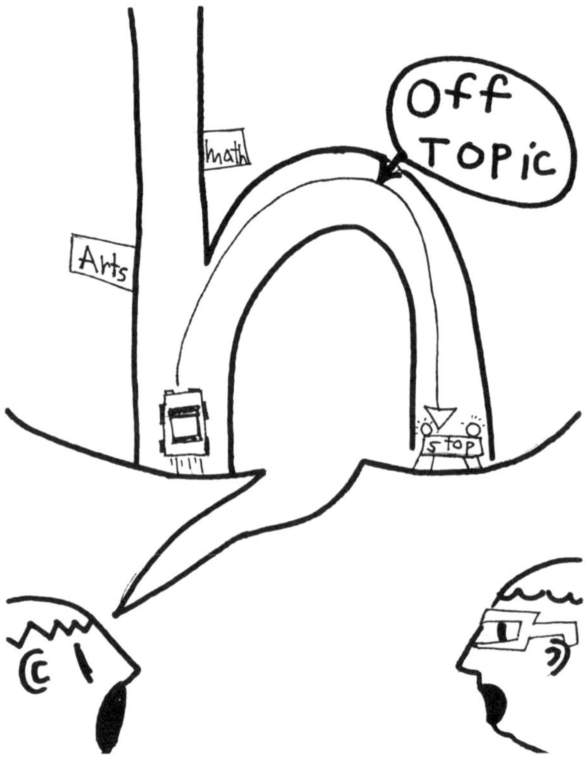

To resist calling out and disturbing the others, Bob can remember these things: Know what the focus of the conversation is, and stop before blurting out in class. Bob can then think if what he has to say is related to the topic and on the Relevance Radar—if it is, then he should raise his hand and wait to be called on by the teacher before he speaks; if it isn't, he should wait until after class to speak to the teacher about it.

Bob wants people to like him, and he wants to be polite to his classmates, so he decides to work hard on not blurting out in school and staying on the topic the group is on. After all, he is very smart and learns quickly. Why not try something new?

2b) Have the students answer comprehension questions.

The answers should resemble the following:

MODULE 3 READING COMPREHENSION SHEET

1. What was the visual support? Select one.

2. Who was the story about? Select one.

○ Al ○ Pat ○ Brad ☒ Bob ○ Freddy ○ Tanya ○ Ricky

3. What was his or her problem? Select one.
   - ○ Didn't control anger
   - ○ Got upset over a change
   - ○ Didn't listen to the teacher
   - ○ Didn't get included
   - ☒ Interrupted the class
   - ○ Didn't know how to handle being teased
   - ○ Focused on others and not on self

4. What did he or she learn to do about it? Write your answer.

   Bob learned to think about whether what he had to say was relevant to the topic before speaking. He learned that if what he had to say was relevant, he should raise his hand and speak when called on, but if what he had to say was not relevant, he should wait and speak to the teacher about it after class.

5. Draw or summarize the story.

   Bob used to ask the teacher many questions and blurt out in class. He didn't understand that when he interrupted the teacher, he was interrupting the learning for others, too. He learned to consider his Relevance Radar before raising his hand.

STEP 3. *MODEL AND REHEARSE.*

3a) Model not staying on topic.

1. Ask a student to reread "Blurting Bob" to the class.

2. Tell students to raise their hands when they hear a blurting comment.

3. When the reader begins, hold up your hand and interrupt the reader by saying, "I have a cousin named Bob." Interrupt or make four irrelevant comments to provide four trials to be labeled.

4. Stop the reader within a few seconds of this point. Provide feedback for those who identified your blurt, or prompt students to raise their hands. Indicate that your statement was outside the topic of the story and therefore an interruption to the reading.

   Note: If you do not have a student in your group who is able to read the story, pick a student to help you model. Direct the student to blurt out "I have a cousin named Bob" at a certain point while you read the story.
   Have students record their score on Line A of the Self-Monitoring Data Sheet.

3b) Rehearse resisting blurting in a contrived manner.

1. Instruct the students to listen to you read or sing quietly.

2. Read or sing a common poem or song that the students would know well enough to complete the words when you entice them to correct or complete your sentence by either stating the words incorrectly or dropping off the last words. For example, say "I pledge allegiance to the...." Instruct the students NOT to complete your sentence verbally but to resist this contrived situation. They can show that they can identify the urge to blurt out the answer by raising their hands instead of completing your phrase.

3. Reinforce this concept to the students who keep quiet by telling them they did a great job refraining from speaking and directing them to record their score on Line B of the Self-Monitoring Data Sheet.

STEP 4. *ROLE-PLAY AND REINFORCE.*

4a) Have the students role-play staying on topic.

1. Place the students in pairs.

2. Have the students pick a single topic to discuss.

3. Instruct each pair to have a conversation in front of the group demonstrating that they can stay on topic.

4. Have peers identify whether the pair remained on topic by showing "thumbs up" or "thumbs down."

5. Provide feedback for each performance.

4b) Prompt the students to mark their data on Line C of the Self-Monitoring Data Sheet.

I can role-play staying on topic with a peer

◯ by myself ◯ with peer help ◯ with teacher help

STEP 5. *PROMOTE GENERALIZATION.*

Appendix B

Send home the Parent Follow-Up Page.

Follow-up directions are provided on the Parent Follow-Up Page.

LESSON 3B

PAYING ATTENTION

STEP 1. *EXPLAIN THE GOAL AND VISUAL SUPPORT.*

1a) Goal

The goal of this lesson is for students to practice paying attention to the teacher and class and to further understand group dynamics. Paying attention to the teacher requires that students stay focused and follow along.

1b) Visual Support

A trail marker tells hikers where they are on a given path and where they need to go to stay on the right path. This lesson uses the Trail Marker tool to help students say, "I'm lost," or stop and ask, "I'm sorry, what did you say?" when they are not following along with the instruction.

1c) Hand out Module 3, Lesson 3B Self-Monitoring Data Sheets to the students.

Provide all lesson handouts for the students to follow through with the remaining steps.

STEP 2. *READ THE SOCIAL COMPASS STORY.*

2a) Read "Pat Likes to Pretend."

Pat likes to pretend. Pat likes movies. Pat likes to pretend he is in the movies. His favorite movies are about magic and monsters. Sometimes he can't tell if something is real or pretend.

Sometimes Pat daydreams about the movies. When someone interrupts his day-dreaming, he feels bad. Sometimes he gets in trouble for not paying attention to the people who are really there and talking to him. He may get the answer wrong in class—or, even worse, he may miss his turn on the computer!

When Pat gets distracted by his thoughts about pretend things, he can think about his Trail Marker tool. If he is listening to the teacher, then he is following the map that his teacher has given; if he is thinking about his favorite movies or something his teacher is not talking about, then he is not following the map! If he is not on the map, he can ask the teacher to help get back on track by asking, "I'm sorry, what did you say?" Then the teacher can repeat what she said, and Pat can make sure he is doing what the teacher expects him to do. He can also be sure to

—Look at her when she begins to speak

—Keep his hands free from materials

—Look at any materials the teacher is talking about

—Ask questions if he is not sure what to do

This makes the teacher happy. This makes Pat happy too.

After he pays attention to the teacher, he can have time to be creative on his own. Pat likes to draw pictures about his favorite movies during his creative time. Everyone can enjoy his imagination when he draws pictures.

2b) Have the students answer comprehension questions.
The answers should resemble the following:

MODULE 3 READING COMPREHENSION SHEET

1. What was the visual support? Select one.

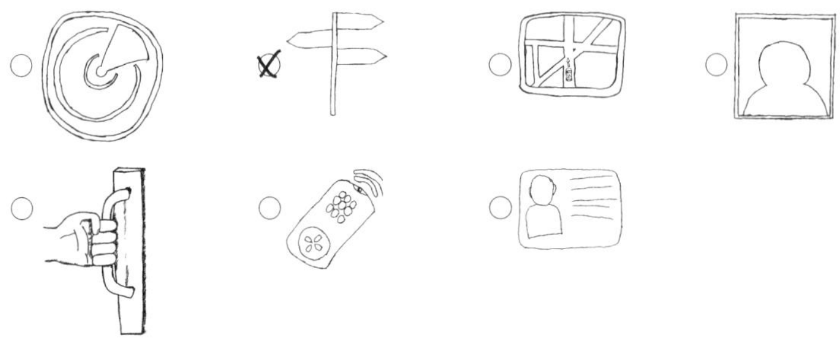

2. Who was the story about? Select one.
   ○ Al ☒ Pat ○ Brad ○ Bob ○ Freddy ○ Tanya ○ Ricky

3. What was his or her problem? Select one.
   - ◯ Didn't control anger
   - ◯ Got upset over a change
   - ☒ Didn't listen to the teacher
   - ◯ Didn't get included
   - ◯ Interrupted the class
   - ◯ Didn't know how to handle being teased
   - ◯ Focused on others and not on self

4. What did he or she learn to do about it? Write your answer.

   Pat learned to pay attention when the teacher is speaking.

5. Draw or summarize the story.

   Pat daydreams during class and gets lost in his thoughts. He can remember his Trail Marker to get back on the path with class. He can say, "I'm sorry, what did you say?" when the teacher calls on him.

STEP 3. *MODEL AND REHEARSE.*

3a) Model not paying attention.

Have a student join you in front of the class. Have him or her start talking to you while you look around, not paying attention. When the student tries to get your attention, say, "What?" Refer to the Trail Marker as a reminder to pay attention when someone is speaking to you.

3b) Have the students rehearse paying attention.

1. Play "Simon Says" using simple directions you can observe (e.g., "Raise your hand if you are wearing a blue shirt").

2. Try several examples, and give students feedback on their performance.

3. Remind students about the Trail Marker for prompts to listen and get back on the right path.

3c) Prompt the students to mark their data on Line A of the Self-Monitoring Data Sheet.

I can play the "Simon Says" game correctly

◯ by myself ◯ with peer help ◯ with teacher help

STEP 4. *ROLE-PLAY AND REINFORCE.*

4a) Have the students role-play paying attention.

As a group, have students role-play behaviors that give the appearance of paying attention: looking at the speaker, leaning forward, and keeping their hands free of materials.

1. Place the students in pairs.
2. Let each pair choose a conversation topic and practice paying attention to each other.
3. Prompt students to use the attention skills noted previously during the conversation.
4. Praise each student for using appropriate behaviors to pay attention.

4b) Prompt the students to mark Lines B1, B2, and B3 of the Self-Monitoring Data Sheet.

I role-played paying attention during a conversation by looking at the speaker, keeping my hands empty, and keeping my body facing the speaker

○ by myself ○ with peer help ○ with teacher help

STEP 5. *PROMOTE GENERALIZATION*

Appendix B

Send home the Parent Follow-Up Page.

Follow-up directions are provided on the Parent Follow-Up Page.

LESSON 3C

ACCEPTING CHANGE IN ROUTINES

STEP 1. *EXPLAIN THE GOAL AND VISUAL SUPPORT.*

1a) Goal

A change in routine can be very upsetting and disruptive for some children. The goal of this lesson is to have students practice how to effectively handle changes in routines.

1b) Visual Support

On most GPS devices, an alert pops up when the user deviates from the suggested route and changes course. Typically, clicking an "accept" button allows the user to continue to be guided by the map. The visual support for this lesson is the GPS Alert, which will help students accept change and move on with their routines.

Appendix A Appendix B

1c) Hand out Module 3, Lesson 3C Self-Monitoring Data Sheets to the students.

Provide all lesson handouts for the students to follow through with the remaining steps.

STEP 2. *READ THE SOCIAL COMPASS STORY.*

2a) Read "Ricky Rides the Bus."

Ricky rides the bus to and from school every week day. Ricky likes knowing what is going to happen each time he gets on the bus. He knows the bus routine.

When he rides the bus, he knows that he should wait quietly in the bus line, say hello to the bus driver, always sit down in the seat on the bus, use his inside voice, and keep his hands and feet to himself. He also knows what time the bus comes to his house and gets to the school each day. Ricky knows when the bus will come back to school to pick him up and take him back home at the end of the day.

One day, there was a change in the bus routine because the bus driver was sick, so there was a substitute driver. The substitute driver is different from the bus driver that Ricky knows and not part of the usual routine. On this day, the substitute bus driver took more time than Ricky's usual bus driver to find her way to the school. After standing in line for a long time with everyone else, Ricky knew his routine was going to be different, but he did not know why. Ricky had a tantrum; he screamed and cried. He scared the other kids who were also waiting for the bus.

The next day, Ricky's teacher told him that when there is a change of plans, or change in his routine, he can picture in his mind an alert going off on his GPS Alert tool. She told him to picture an alert button on his GPS when routines change. The alert button will let him know there has been a change in plans, and he can then push the "accept" button to help him relax. He can take a deep breath, remember that he will get home soon, and enjoy the trip home.

2b) Have the students answer comprehension questions.

The answers should resemble the following:

MODULE 3 READING COMPREHENSION SHEET

1. What was the visual support? Select one.

○  ○  ☒  ○ 

○ 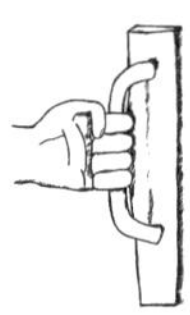 ○  ○ 

2. Who was the story about? Select one.

○ Al ○ Pat ○ Brad ○ Bob ○ Freddy ○ Tanya ☒ Ricky

3. What was his or her problem? Select one.
   - ○ Didn't control anger
   - ☒ Got upset over a change
   - ○ Didn't listen to the teacher
   - ○ Didn't get included
   - ○ Interrupted the class
   - ○ Didn't know how to handle being teased
   - ○ Focused on others and not on self

4. What did he or she learn to do about it? Write your answer.

   He learned to accept the change and enjoy the ride.

5. Draw or summarize the story.

   Ricky got upset when the bus routine changed. He learned to stay calm by remembering his GPS Alert visual and accept the change.

STEP 3. *MODEL AND REHEARSE.*

3a) Model why coping with change is important.

1. Provide an immediate example of a change, and model strategies to cope with that change. Explain to the students that coping with change is important because change happens so frequently everyone needs to be prepared for it.
2. Announce that the students' chairs are not to be used and everyone needs to sit on the floor immediately.
3. Point to the GPS Alert visual icon to indicate a change is happening and the students should accept it and move on with the new activity.
4. Praise students who follow through without complaint or hesitation. Have the students label strategies for coping with change. Ask students to label strategies to try when asked to change. Examples include staying calm and following through with sitting on the floor.
5. Direct students to record their data on Line A of the Self-Monitoring Data Sheet.

3b) Have students rehearse making changes by having them change their seats.

1. Have the students walk around the room until you say, "Sit."
2. As they go to sit in their seats, change the rule about how or where they should sit by saying, "Sit one chair to the left of your (usual) seat."

3. Provide feedback on students' ability to adapt to last-minute change in directions. Then, have them walk around the room again, and when it's time for them to sit down, try another change such as "Sit on your chair backwards" or "Sit on the floor next to your chair."
4. Give feedback about the students' ability to follow through with these changes.
5. Praise them for accepting the changes, and point to the GPS Alert icon to prompt accepting the change.

3) Prompt the students to mark their data on Line B for each of the previous trials on the Self-Monitoring Data Sheet.

I can rehearse making changes in a group game format of musical chairs

◯ by myself ◯ with peer help ◯ with teacher help

STEP 4. *ROLE-PLAY AND REINFORCE.*

4a) Have the students role-play accepting a change in their routines.

1. Place the students in pairs.
2. Have the students practice accepting a change in their routines by notifying each other about various changes (e.g., their teacher is absent, their parent can't pick them up from school that day, they need to move their seats to the back of class, they can't go outside for recess that day).
3. The partner receiving the news responds to it by accepting the change and going along with it.
4. Solicit feedback from each pair after they role-play in front of the class, and solicit feedback from the observers as well. Be sure each student has an opportunity to play the role of the person who needs to accept a change in plans.

4b) Prompt the students to mark their data on Line C of the Self-Monitoring Data Sheet.

I was able to accept a change in my routine in role play with a peer

◯ by myself ◯ with peer help ◯ with teacher help

STEP 5. *PROMOTE GENERALIZATION.*

Appendix B

Send home the Parent Follow-Up Page.

Follow-up directions are provided on the Parent Follow-Up Page.

LESSON 3D
RESISTING TATTLING

STEP 1. *EXPLAIN THE GOAL AND VISUAL SUPPORT.*

1a) Goal

Most children are curious about what others around them are doing. As they develop a sense of what is right and wrong, children tend to tattle on others, or express tiny infractions to an enforcer to demonstrate their knowledge. When there is a serious situation that requires an adult to intervene, however, this is not tattling. Be sure to explain the difference between needing an adult for serious situations and reporting minor infractions.

When a child reports a peer or sibling's infraction to an adult instead of attempting to resolve the issue with the other person, it is often considered by the adult to be tattling. Tattling is perceived as an attempt by the student to gain attention from the adult, which takes away from the child's positive interaction with the other person. The goal of this lesson is to have students practice how to resist tattling.

1b) Visual Support

A self-portrait is a picture of oneself drawn by oneself. It is focused on the artist and only the artist. This lesson uses the Self-Portrait tool as the visual support to remind students to focus on themselves and their performance (i.e., mind their own business), not on others (unless they ask for feedback).

1c) Hand out Module 3, Lesson 3D Self-Monitoring Data Sheets to the students.

Appendix A Appendix B

Provide all lesson handouts for the students to follow through with the remaining steps.

STEP 2. *READ THE SOCIAL COMPASS STORY.*

2a) Read "Tanya Tries Not to Tattle."

Tanya really likes middle school and is great in science and math. When it comes to hanging with the gang, though, Tanya is not so hot. One time Tanya had to do a group project in science. She wanted to do it by herself because she felt she knew all the

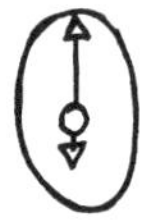

facts about geology and could even spell every mountain range correctly. But when Tanya sat with her group, she was annoyed that her buddy couldn't spell *Mount Rushmore*. Her buddy spelled the word *Mount Rushmoor*. Tanya wanted it spelled correctly and she knew the right way to spell it. She blurted out, "Hey, Teacher, he spelled a word wrong!" This statement embarrassed her classmate. His jaw dropped open and his eyes widened; Tanya's buddy was really bummed out. Tanya's teacher told her, "Tanya, that's his work; don't worry about it." Her teacher told her that she needs to focus on herself and not on what other people are doing. To help Tanya remember to do this, her teacher told her to use her imaginary Self-Portrait tool as a reminder that all Tanya has to worry about is herself and that she should mind her own business. Tanya understood that she had hurt her classmate's feelings by pointing out his spelling mistake. Being told a person is wrong in public can make someone feel stupid.

The next day in the group when Tanya saw her buddy spell another word wrong she said, "I've never seen that word spelled that way before. Should we look it up?" This was a cool way for Tanya to find out if her friend wanted help. When her friend said, "Nah, thanks anyway," Tanya remembered her Self-Portrait and thought to herself, "Oh well, that's his choice, and that's okay." Tanya was beginning to learn to mind her own business and be a good friend.

2b) Have the students answer comprehension questions.

The answers should resemble the following:

MODULE 3 READING COMPREHENSION SHEET

1. What was the visual support? Select one.

2. Who was the story about? Select one.

○ Al ○ Pat ○ Brad ○ Bob ○ Freddy ☒ Tanya ○ Ricky

3. What was his or her problem? Select one.
   - ◯ Didn't control anger
   - ◯ Got upset over a change
   - ◯ Didn't listen to the teacher
   - ◯ Didn't get included
   - ◯ Interrupted the class
   - ◯ Didn't know how to handle being teased
   - ☒ Focused on others and not on self

4. What did he or she learn to do about it? Write your answer.

   Tanya learned to focus on herself and not point out others' mistakes.

5. Draw or summarize the story.

   Tanya points out what her friend is doing wrong in front of a group of people. Tanya's buddy gets his feelings hurt. Tanya learned to mind her own business.

STEP 3. *MODEL AND REHEARSE.*

3a) Model when to resist tattling by labeling sample scenarios.

Have students write the correct way to respond to each of the following activities on Line A of the Self-Monitoring Data Sheet. The correct answers are shown in bold print.

1. A classmate is eating her snack too early.

   Tell the teacher.
   Ignore it and focus on you.
   Tell the student the classroom rules.

2. An older student hurt someone on the playground.

   Tell the teacher.
   Ignore it and focus on you.
   Tell the student the classroom rules.

3. A classmate is not reading his book during reading time.

   Tell the teacher.
   Ignore it and focus on you.
   Tell the student the classroom rules.

4. A classmate is picking her nose.

   Tell the teacher.
   Ignore it and focus on you.
   Tell the student the classroom rules.

3b) Have the students rehearse by using sample cards.

Have the whole group of students rehearse focusing on their own behavior and resisting tattling during a manufactured opportunity. The following example is related to the teacher being distracted from the group to answer the phone.

1. Have a selected student implement instructions that are written on a card and handed to him or her as the activity begins. The sample cards might contain these activities for that student to present: whisper to your neighbor, take your neighbor's book from him, pretend to be chewing gum, pretend to gently poke your neighbor.
2. Instruct the other students to raise their hands when they see an opportunity to tattle but are resisting doing so.

3c) Prompt students to complete data for Line B on the Self-Monitoring Data Sheet.

I can rehearse resisting tattling by raising my hand when an opportunity for tattling occurred

○ by myself ○ with peer help ○ with teacher help

STEP 4. *ROLE-PLAY AND REINFORCE.*

4a) Have the students role-play resisting tattling.

Have students role-play different situations in which tattling could occur but doesn't, such as the following:

—A student looks at someone else's answers during a spelling test.
—A student takes someone else's pencil out of his or her desk.
—A student says a bad word.
—A student calls someone else a silly name.
—A student has a forbidden item such as candy.

4b) Prompt the students to mark their data on Line C of the Self-Monitoring Data Sheet.

I can role-play not tattling during a structured activity

○ by myself ○ with peer help ○ with teacher help

STEP 5. *PROMOTE GENERALIZATION.*

Appendix B

Send home the Parent Follow-Up Page.

Follow-up directions are provided on the Parent Follow-Up Page.

LESSON 3E
HANDLING TEASING

STEP 1. *EXPLAIN THE GOAL AND VISUAL SUPPORT.*

1a) Goal

There are subtle differences in the ways students talk with each other and joke around together, and many times teasing is meant to be good-natured. This type of friendly joking, however, can sometimes change into uncomfortable situations. The goal of this lesson is for students to learn how to handle teasing, regardless of the other person's intentions. Teasing behavior can border on bullying, so it is important to stress to students that bullying is not acceptable behavior and that they should be very aware of how someone feels when he or she gets teased. The moment someone becomes uncomfortable or the comments are unwelcomed, teasing is no longer friendly.

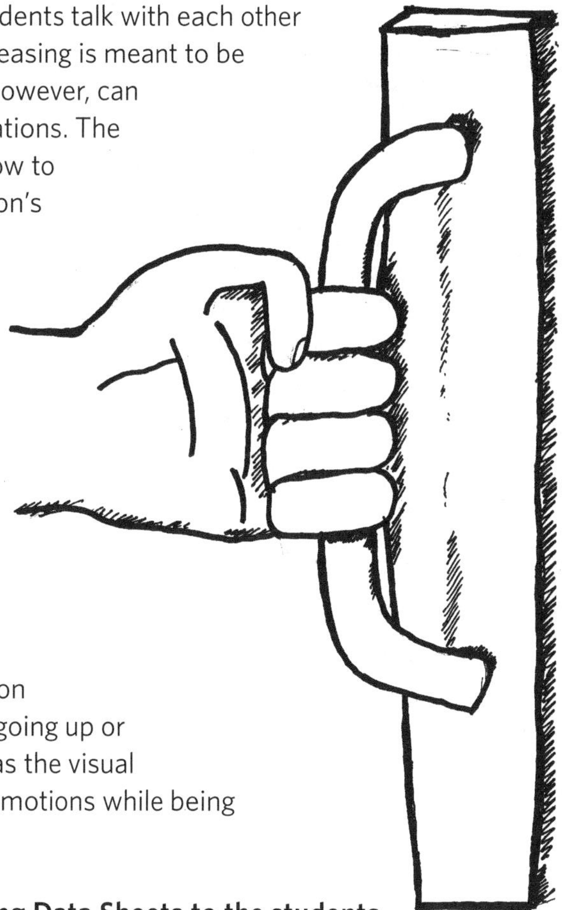

1b) Visual Support

A handle is a tool that is attached to many objects so that people can get a better grip on something, such as the handle on a bus for going up or down the stairs. This lesson uses a Handle as the visual reminder for students to "hold on" to their emotions while being teased.

1c) Hand out Module 3, Lesson 3E Self-Monitoring Data Sheets to the students.

Provide all lesson handouts for the students to follow through with the remaining steps.

STEP 2. *READ THE SOCIAL COMPASS STORY.*

2a) Read "Freddy's Friendly Teasing."

At school, there are many students. Some classmates are friendly to each other. Sometimes they are unfriendly and tease each other. It is hard to understand all the ways friends tease each other and what it means. Sometimes friends tease in a friendly

way because they like to have some fun. They make jokes that include others to make everyone laugh. Sometimes the joke is about Freddy. When friends are teasing Freddy in a friendly way, he often laughs and gently teases them back. Some teasing can be really funny; everyone laughs and then people tell more jokes to make their friends happy. Teasing is friendly when it is funny to everyone. But sometimes teasing is not funny, especially if it is done in a mean way and hurts someone's feelings. Freddy remembers that it is never okay to tease about things that hurt other people's feelings. Unfriendly teasing can be about things such as death, disease, disabilities, and poverty. These aren't funny. This teasing is unkind. Some teasing is hard to understand and makes people feel uncomfortable.

If the teasing or joke isn't funny to Freddy, he can say, "That's not funny," or just walk away.

If it is too hard for Freddy to understand what the other kids are saying or if it makes him feel uncomfortable, Freddy can walk away or say something such as "Hey, I don't get it," or "That's really not funny."

Using one of these strategies will let the person who is doing the teasing or joking know how Freddy feels on the inside. And if they don't mean to hurt Freddy's feelings, they should stop the teasing or joking.

If they don't stop, Freddy may go from feeling a little embarrassed to feeling really mad. This is a difficult emotion to handle when Freddy is with his friends. To make himself feel better, Freddy can use his imaginary Handle. He can imagine himself staying on his feet and in control by placing his hand on the "handle" of his emotions. This can help Freddy handle the teasing and mean jokes. He then can change the topic of the conversation by saying something such as, "Hey, tell me something about you for a change." Or Freddy can leave the situation—he can go read a book or start a conversation with someone else who is not going to tease him, for example. Freddy also can say to himself, "They are only trying to make me laugh, so I'm going to laugh with them."

2b) Have the students answer comprehension questions.

The answers should resemble the following:

MODULE 3 READING COMPREHENSION SHEET

1. What was the visual support? Select one.

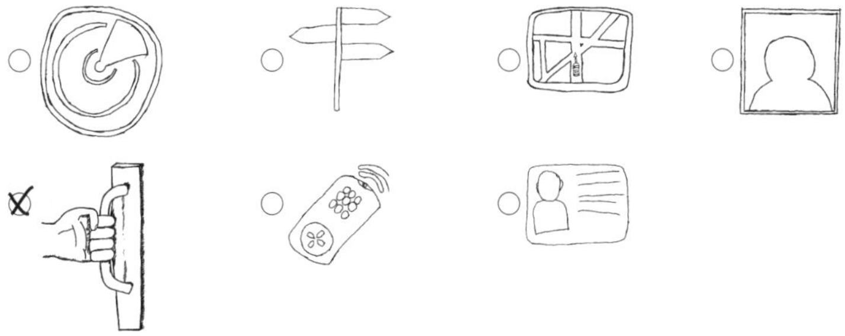

2. Who was the story about? Select one.
   ○ Al ○ Pat ○ Brad ○ Bob ☒ Freddy ○ Tanya ○ Ricky

3. What was his or her problem? Select one.
   - ○ Didn't control anger
   - ○ Got upset over a change
   - ○ Didn't listen to the teacher
   - ○ Didn't get included
   - ○ Interrupted the class
   - ☒ Didn't know how to handle being teased
   - ○ Focused on others and not on self

4. What did he or she learn to do about it? Write your answer.
   He learned to "hold on" to his feelings and decide if the teasing was friendly or unfriendly.

5. Draw or summarize the story.
   Freddy learned there is good and bad teasing and what to do about each.

STEP 3. *MODEL AND REHEARSE.*

3a) Model how to handle teasing.

1. Pick a partner to say to you, in front of the whole class, remarks that are not friendly. Provide four examples, such as "Hey, your hair looks funny," "Your shoes are ugly," "You have the worst breath," and "You like (a peer's name)."
2. Hold up your Handle visual support.
3. Decide out loud that that you will reply to this comment by saying, "Whatever!", "Oh, well," or "Sorry you feel that way," or by just walking away.
4. Have students label if you showed a good or bad response for each trial on Line A of the Self-Monitoring Data Sheet.

3b) Have the students rehearse responding to teasing.

1. Place the students in pairs to practice simultaneously. Monitor each group and provide feedback.
2. Have one of the students make a teasing remark to the other such as, "Your hair looks funny," "Your shoes are ugly," or "You did terribly on that test."
3. Have the other partner respond with a recently practiced or scripted response such as, "I know—bad hair day!" "Sorry to hear you don't like my shoes," or "Oh, well, better luck next time."

3c) Prompt the students to mark their rehearsal data on Line B on the Self-Monitoring Data Sheet.

I can use scripts to handle teasing

◯ by myself ◯ with peer help ◯ with teacher help

STEP 4. *ROLE-PLAY AND REINFORCE.*

4a) Have the student pairs role-play as one pair at a time handling teasing appropriately.

1. Place the students in pairs.
2. Have each pair get up in front of the class and provide gentle insults to each other.
3. Have the rest of the class raise their hands when the students who are role-playing need to handle teasing.
4. Have the student being teased in the role play say a unique or scripted response.
5. Have the rest of the class give a "thumbs up" when they see a good strategy being used.
6. Provide prompts to assist the students when they are not demonstrating appropriate skills.

4b) Prompt the students to mark their data on Line C of the Self-Monitoring Data Sheet.

I can use my own statements to handle teasing

◯ by myself ◯ with peer help ◯ with teacher help

STEP 5. *PROMOTE GENERALIZATION.*

Appendix B

Send home the Parent Follow-Up Page.

Follow-up directions are provided on the Parent Follow-Up Page.

LESSON 3F

USING SELF-CONTROL

STEP 1. *EXPLAIN THE GOAL AND VISUAL SUPPORT.*

1a) Goal

The escalation from being a little upset to becoming out of control can happen quickly for some students. The goal of this lesson is to have students recognize and understand the onset of intense emotions and practice staying in control.

1b) Visual Support

The visual support for this lesson is a Self-Controller remote control with the buttons "Stop," "Slow Down," and "Go." These buttons are meant to remind students how to manage or control their own behavior.

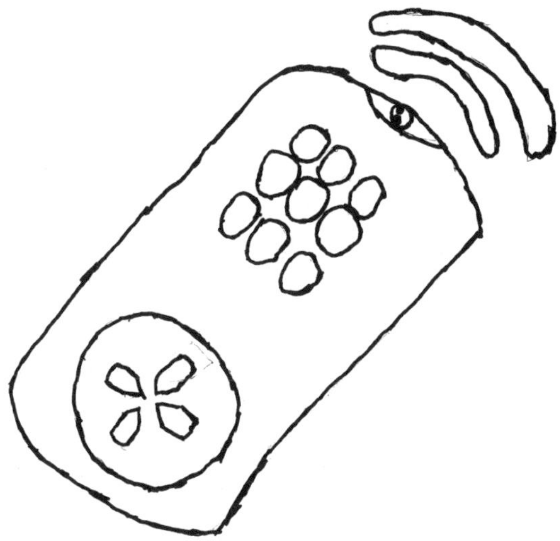

Appendix A Appendix B

1c) Hand out Module 3, Lesson 3F Self-Monitoring Data Sheets to the students.

Provide all lesson handouts for the students to follow through with the remaining steps.

STEP 2. *READ THE SOCIAL COMPASS STORY.*

2a) Read "Al Gets Angry."

Al gets good grades most of the time. Sometimes, it is hard for him to listen to all the directions that the teacher gives. Sometimes Al gets confused in class and forgets to raise his hand when he gets lost. One time he missed the class instruction and was embarrassed. He was immediately angry. Al began to throw pencils and yell. He was not thinking about the other students. His teacher had to stop everything she was doing with the whole class to calm him down.

The next day, Al had to talk to the principal. She told Al to imagine that he had a Self-Controller that looked like a remote control but with only three buttons: a red, "Stop" button, a yellow "Slow Down" button, and a green "Go" button. Then she explained that Al could use special areas or zones in his classroom and school to help with his anger. She said that when he starts to lose control, he could envision his "Slow

Down" button and go sit in a yellow zone in the classroom. The yellow zone is a place to go so he can slow down his anger. The principal suggested using a special chair in a quiet area of the classroom. When Al feels out of control he can envision his "Stop" button and go to a red zone away from what made him feel out of control and outside of the busy classroom to stop his anger. Al and the principal decided he could use a quiet area in the principal's office as his red zone. The principal said that when things are going fine and Al feels in control, it's like pushing the green "Go" button on his controller. This is the time to keep working, be with his classmates, and ask the teacher a question.

During an activity the following day, Al missed the teacher's instruction and started to feel confused and hot inside. Instead of yelling and throwing things, Al remembered to use his Self-Controller: He imagined himself pushing the yellow "Slow Down" button, and he went to a special chair in the yellow zone of the classroom. In a short time, about a minute, his teacher came by and waited for him to ask for help. Al said, "I am confused. What am I supposed to be doing right now?" The teacher explained the task to Al again. Al was in control now and he moved back to his own seat. He was back in the green zone. Al was learning to have self-control.

2b) Have the students answer comprehension questions.

The answers should resemble the following:

MODULE 3 READING COMPREHENSION SHEET

1. What was the visual support? Select one.

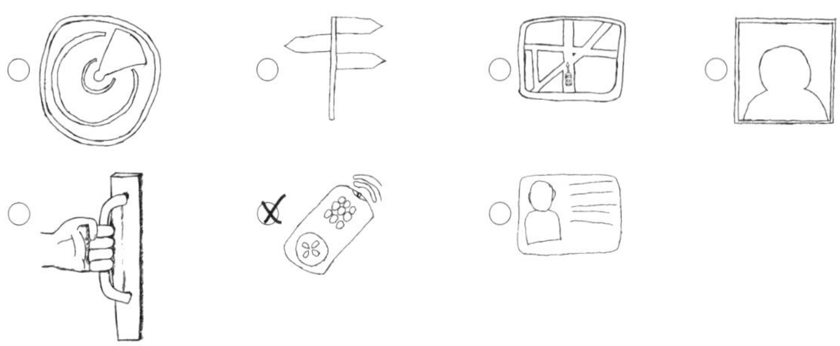

2. Who was the story about? Select one.

☒ Al ○ Pat ○ Brad ○ Bob ○ Freddy ○ Tanya ○ Ricky

3. What was his or her problem? Select one.
   - ☒ Didn't control anger
   - ○ Got upset over a change
   - ○ Didn't listen to the teacher
   - ○ Didn't get included
   - ○ Interrupted the class
   - ○ Didn't know how to handle being teased
   - ○ Focused on others and not on self

4. What did he or she learn to do about it? Write your answer.

   Al learned to push his Self-Controller to slow down before he got too angry and to stop himself from getting out of control.

5. Draw or summarize the story.

   Al got angry and threw pencils. He got in trouble. The principal taught him to slow down before he gets out of control.

STEP 3. *MODEL AND REHEARSE.*

3a) Model how to control anger.

Act out the following scenario in front of your class:

1. You receive a phone call telling you that your car has just been wrecked.
2. Demonstrate agitated behaviors (e.g., grimacing, stomping feet, making fists), then pause and hit the red "Stop" button on your Self-Controller.
3. Have the students identify the behaviors you just modeled as being angry. Have students indicate their response on Line A of the Self-Monitoring Data Sheet.
4. Have the students explain why staying in control is important.

3b) Have the students rehearse how to control anger.

1. Have the students, as a whole group, imitate getting angry and calming themselves down just as you modeled.
2. Encourage them to use their Self-Controllers and the strategies discussed in the Social Compass story.

3c) Prompt the students to mark their data on Line B of the Self-Monitoring Data Sheet.

I can rehearse being angry without displaying aggressive behavior

○ by myself ○ with peer help ○ with teacher help

STEP 4. *ROLE-PLAY AND REINFORCE.*

4a) Have the students role-play using self-control.

1. Place the students in pairs and have them role-play a conflict of their choosing in front of the rest of the class. For students who need some ideas, suggest one of the following: a classmate takes something that belongs to them (e.g., seat, place in line, materials for a project), a favorite event is cancelled (e.g., movie night, play date), they get punished, or they feel like they received an unfair grade on a test or project.
2. Direct them to use their Self-Controllers and find a positive resolution.
3. Have the rest of the class label specific behaviors they observe in others' examples, such as not stomping, not yelling, not grimacing, or pretending to push the stop button on their Self-Controllers.
4. Provide prompts to assist the students when they are not demonstrating appropriate skills.
5. Provide feedback to each student on his or her performance during the role plays.

4b) Prompt the students to mark their data on Line C of the Self-Monitoring Data Sheet.

I can role-play a conflict without losing control and make a positive choice to resolve it

○ by myself ○ with peer help ○ with teacher help

STEP 5. *PROMOTE GENERALIZATION.*

Appendix B

Send home the Parent Follow-Up Page.

Follow-up directions are provided on the Parent Follow-Up Page.

LESSON 3G

AVOIDING BEING LEFT OUT

STEP 1. *EXPLAIN THE GOAL AND VISUAL SUPPORT.*

1a) Goal

Throughout most of a student's school career, being included in a group is critically important. Although it may not always be something they can control, students can try some strategies to be a part of things, or not to be left out. The goal of this lesson is to have students practice how to avoid being left out.

1b) Visual Support

Many groups use membership cards as a physical representation of being part of their group. Some examples of membership cards are those for a fitness center and a warehouse club. If someone feels alone or separate from the group, he or she can seek out membership in a group. Groups accept new members who are interested in being a part of the group and willing to follow the rules. Groups may have rules, some written and some not written, about the specific type of behavior they expect from their members. Observing and adhering to these rules of membership is a skill required for joining and staying part of any group. This lesson uses the Membership Card tool to remind students to think about the rules of a group to avoid being left out.

Appendix A Appendix B

1c) Hand out Module 3, Lesson 3G Self-Monitoring Data Sheets to the students.

Provide all lesson handouts for the students to follow through with the remaining steps.

STEP 2. *READ THE SOCIAL COMPASS STORY.*

2a) Read "Brad Was a Bully."

Brad is the biggest boy in his class. Brad believes he is the king of the class. Of course, he is not, but he thinks he is! At recess, he likes to tell everybody what to do. He likes to be the first to take a turn at each new game. The other kids think he is a bully. One day, the other kids decided to let him have his way. They let him pick all the games and go first. At first, Brad thought this was great. But, when it was their time to take a turn, they all sat down and said, "I quit." Brad had no one to bully. This wasn't fun at all. Brad felt disrespected.

He felt what the others felt each time he bullied them, and he didn't like it one bit. To have fun playing games means to respect each person. The next day Brad decided to watch and see how the others played together. He saw that they respected each other by

—Never making fun at someone's mistake
—Never being mean on purpose
—Never lying or blaming someone else for their mistake

He also saw that they
—Didn't get upset if they lost the game or didn't go first
—Said, "I'm sorry" if they hurt someone
—Really enjoyed just being together

Brad imagined himself applying for membership. He realized he had not shown his interest in belonging and that if he wanted to be included in games, he had to show his Membership Card to indicate that he wanted to be included in the group and agreed to the rules. At the end of recess, Brad joined the group and offered to carry in the equipment. He said out loud, "I am no longer going to be Brad the Bully. I am going to be Brad the Buddy!" Everyone smiled and gave him high fives. Brad felt great. Being friends is better than being a bully!

2b) Have the students answer comprehension questions.

The answers should resemble the following:

MODULE 3 READING COMPREHENSION SHEET

1. What was the visual support? Select one.

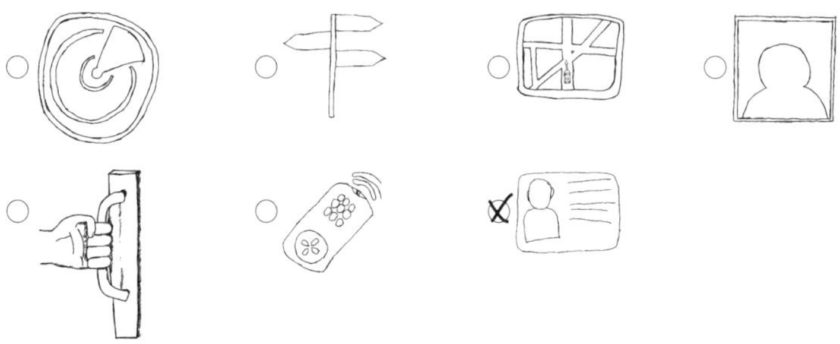

2. Who was the story about? Select one.

○ Al ○ Pat ☒ Brad ○ Bob ○ Freddy ○ Tanya ○ Ricky

3. What was his or her problem? Select one.
   ○ Didn't control anger
   ○ Got upset over a change
   ○ Didn't listen to the teacher
   ☒ Didn't get included
   ○ Interrupted the class
   ○ Didn't know how to handle being teased
   ○ Focused on others and not on self

4. What did he or she learn to do about it? Write your answer.

   Brad learned to show his Membership Card, indicating that he wanted to be included in the group.

5. Draw or summarize the story.

   Brad was bossy and his classmates stopped playing with him. He watched and learned that the classmates showed respect for each other. The students supported each other as a group. He changed his ways and was able to join the group.

STEP 3. *MODEL AND REHEARSE.*

3a) Model how to avoid being left out of a group.

Discuss how it feels to be left out. Model for the students how to remain part of a group by musical chairs. Tell the class you are the one with no seat. Model walking up to someone with a chair, smiling, looking at that person, and asking to join him or her, and then pretend to show your Membership Card. Have students label the behaviors you modeled to show you wanted to join the student on the chair. Have students mark Line A of the Self-Monitoring Data Sheet.

3b) Have the students rehearse avoiding being left out of a group.

1. As the chairs are removed, have the two students closest to the remaining chair share the chair so that they both stay in the game.
2. Prompt students at risk of being left out to raise their hands to "show their Membership Cards" and send a message that they want to be included and not left out of the game.
3. Continue to eliminate chairs until everyone is paired up, and no one is left out.
4. Praise the students' efforts to work together so that no one was excluded.

3c) Prompt the students to mark Line B on the Self-Monitoring Data Sheet.

In a game format, I can work with others to avoid being left out

○ by myself ○ with peer help ○ with teacher help

STEP 4. *ROLE-PLAY AND REINFORCE.*

4a) Have the students role-play how to avoid being left out of a group.

Have the students practice how they can indicate that they want to be part of or join a group.

1. Assign two members of the group to be leaders, and have them alternate picking other members of the class to be a part of their team.
2. Prompt the students to remain active by having them face the leaders and look at them with interest. Have them use their Membership Cards to indicate which team they want to be on.
3. Have peers provide encouragement for anyone raising their hands to communicate that they want to be part of the group.
4. Provide continual feedback and prompting as needed.

4b) Prompt the students to mark Line C on the Self-Monitoring Data Sheet.

I can role-play becoming part of a group

○ by myself ○ with peer help ○ with teacher help

STEP 5. *PROMOTE GENERALIZATION.*

Send home the Parent Follow-Up Page.

Follow-up directions are provided on the Parent Follow-Up Page.

MODULE 4

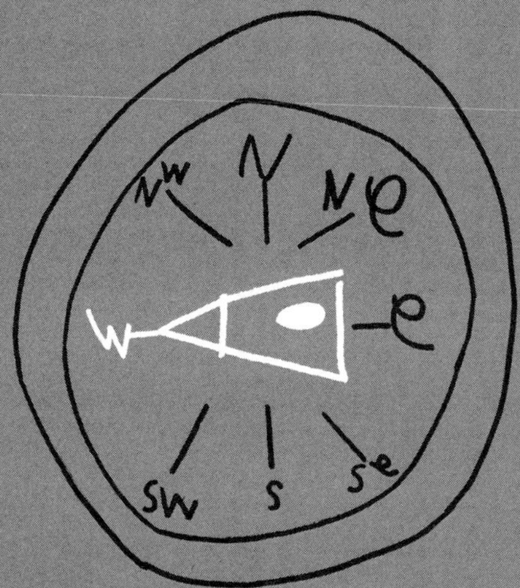

"WE" SKILLS

This module focuses on conversation skills, which this curriculum refers to as "We" skills. Conversations are an inherent part of our lives—so much so that sometimes we do not realize that conversations are multifaceted and that we use complex social skills to engage in them. Many skills are necessary to begin and sustain a successful conversation. This module examines initiating a conversation, asking questions, sharing interests, complimenting your conversation partner, expanding personal interests, paraphrasing, negotiating or balancing the exchange, maintaining the conversation, and knowing when to end it.

The visual supports used to help teach these skills include a Start Button, a Question Bubble, a Display Case, Compliment Confetti, an Interest Inventory, a Paraphrasing Funnel, a Friendship Balance, Conversation Glue, and a Time's-Up Tin.

Module 4 Lessons

4A—INITIATING A CONVERSATION

VISUAL SUPORT: START BUTTON

4B—ASKING QUESTIONS

VISUAL SUPORT: QUESTION BUBBLE

4C—SHARING INFORMATION

VISUAL SUPORT: DISPLAY CASE

4D—GIVING COMPLIMENTS

VISUAL SUPORT: COMPLIMENT CONFETTI

4E—EXPANDING PERSONAL INTERESTS

VISUAL SUPORT: INTEREST INVENTORY

4F—PARAPHRASING

VISUAL SUPORT: PARAPHRASING FUNNEL

4G—NEGOTIATING NEEDS

VISUAL SUPORT: FRIENDSHIP BALANCE

4H—MAINTAINING A CONVERSATION

VISUAL SUPORT: CONVERSATION GLUE

4I—ENDING A CONVERSATION

VISUAL SUPORT: TIME'S-UP TIN

LESSON 4A

INITIATING A CONVERSATION

STEP 1. *EXPLAIN THE GOAL AND VISUAL SUPPORT.*

1a) Goal

The first step to having a conversation is to start one. The goal of this lesson is to have students practice getting involved in activities and starting conversations.

1b) Visual Support

The power button, or start button, on electronics is what gets the device to turn on. Initiating a conversation or joining a group is like pushing a start button—it's what gets the conversation started. This lesson uses the Start Button tool to help students learn how to initiate a conversation so that they can get involved in their desired activity immediately.

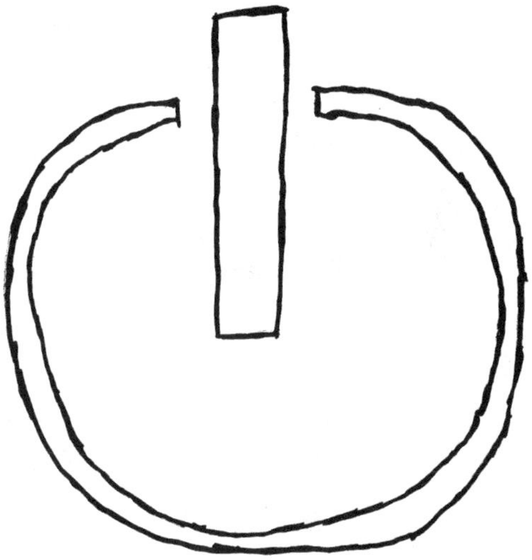

1c) Hand out Module 4, Lesson 4A Self-Monitoring Data Sheets to the students.

Appendix A Appendix B

Provide all lesson handouts for the students to follow through with the remaining steps.

STEP 2. *READ THE SOCIAL COMPASS STORY.*

2a) Read "Ned Gets Nervous."

Ned loves to play basketball. Ned watches the other boys pass the ball at recess and gets excited about the game. He wants to join the group and play ball, too, but he is too nervous to ask to play. He walks up to the group and shows his excitement by hopping up and down. The boys do not know why Ned is hopping and that Ned wants to join in and play ball with them. Some of the boys start to play ball again, and some of them walk away. Ned feels sad that he is left out of the game, but he doesn't know another way to ask the boys to join in.

Ned's teacher sees the boys move away. His teacher explains to him that he is not sharing his message in a way that the boys understand. Ned has a hard time starting conversations. It makes him nervous, and he hops when he gets nervous or excited.

His teacher tells him there is a better way to communicate that he wants to join a game. She tells him he can imagine pushing his Start Button tool in his head and then start the conversation by saying, "Can I play, too?" Ned tries these strategies the next day. After asking, "Can I play, too?" one of the boys throws the ball to Ned, and knows he is in the game too. Ned felt great, and the boys liked that they knew what Ned wanted to do. They can all play ball together now. His teacher was happy, too.

2b) Have the students answer comprehension questions.

The answers should resemble the following:

MODULE 4 READING COMPREHENSION SHEET

1. What was the visual support? Select one.

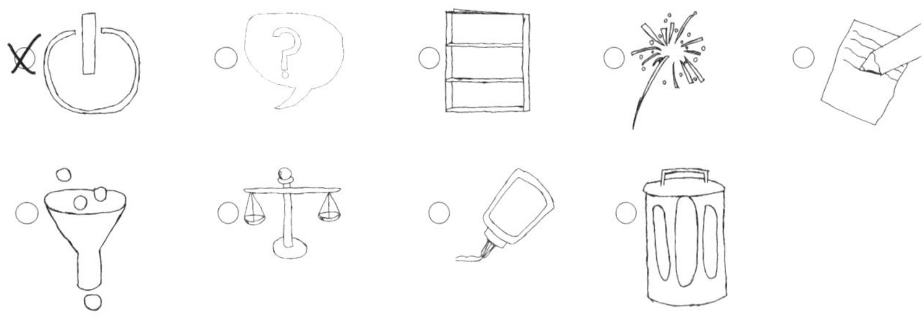

2. Who was the story about? Select one.

○ Willy ○ Evan ○ Connie ○ Alex
○ Sharon ☒ Ned ○ Mike ○ Patrick ○ Frank

3. What was his or her problem? Select one.
   - ○ Didn't know how to compliment someone
   - ○ Didn't know when to stop talking
   - ○ Didn't share knowledge with others
   - X Didn't know how to start a conversation
   - ○ Didn't give friends a turn to talk
   - ○ Didn't know about things others know
   - ○ Didn't get more information
   - ○ Didn't think about what friends like
   - ○ Didn't seem to listen by checking in with the speaker

4. What did he or she learn to do about it? Write your answer.

   Ned learned to initiate a conversation when he wanted to join in the game. Instead of hopping, he stopped and asked if he could play basketball with the other kids.

5. Draw or summarize the story.

   Ned didn't know how to join the game so he hopped up and down. The boys didn't know he wanted to join. When Ned imagined himself pushing his Start Button and said, "Can I play, too?" the other boys said yes and they all played together.

STEP 3. *MODEL AND REHEARSE.*

3a) Model starting a conversation.

1. Refer students to the Start Button visual support.
2. Ask two students to come up and have a conversation in front of the class so that you can model starting a conversation with them.
3. Walk up to the students and say your thoughts out loud (e.g., "Hmmm, I'd like to join this conversation, so I think I am going to imagine pushing my Start Button and ask, 'Hey, what are you guys talking about?'").
4. Approach the students and ask, "Hey, what are you guys talking about?" Have students raise their hands at the moment they believe you successfully joined in. Discuss the behaviors they observed that led to them to select the moment they chose. Give them feedback about the correctness of their choice. Have students mark Line A on their Self-Monitoring Data Sheets.

3b) Have the students rehearse by imitating your model.

1. Place students in groups of three.
2. Have two of the students in each group start a conversation while the third student practices pushing the imaginary Start Button and asks to join the conversation.
3. Have the students rotate whose turn it is to join in the conversation.

3c) Prompt the students to mark Line B on the Self-Monitoring Data Sheet.

I can practice starting a conversation verbally or with a visual support

○ by myself ○ with peer help ○ with teacher help

STEP 4. *ROLE-PLAY AND REINFORCE.*

4a) Have the students role-play beginning a conversation.

1. Place the students in pairs.
2. Have the students choose a conversation topic from a jar of topics. (A list of topics is included in Appendix B and among the accompanying online materials. Cut on the dotted lines to make each topic a strip of paper that can be placed in the jar.)
3. Determine who will begin speaking and start the conversation for each role play.
4. Have the students role-play their conversation (with at least two exchanges) in front of the rest of the class.
5. Verbally prompt the pair role-playing by saying "Start" if there is a delay of 2–5 seconds.
6. Have students identify if the speaker successfully started the conversation by showing "thumbs up" or "thumbs down."

4b) Prompt the students to mark their data on Line C of the Self-Monitoring Data Sheet.

I can start a conversation during a role-play within 5 seconds

○ by myself ○ with peer help ○ with teacher help

STEP 5. *PROMOTE GENERALIZATION.*

Send home the Parent Follow-Up Page.

Follow-up directions are provided on the Parent Follow-Up Page.

LESSON 4B

ASKING QUESTIONS

STEP 1. *EXPLAIN THE GOAL AND VISUAL SUPPORT.*

1a) Goal

It is easy to get sidetracked when talking with someone. One way to avoid getting sidetracked and keep a conversation going is to ask questions. The goal of this lesson is to help students learn how to keep a conversation going by asking questions that are relevant to the conversation.

1b) Visual Support

The visual support for this lesson is a Question Bubble. The Question Bubble serves as a reminder to students that they need to ask questions during conversations.

1c) Hand out Module 4, Lesson 4B Self-Monitoring Data Sheets to the students.

Appendix A Appendix B

Provide all lesson handouts for the students to follow through with the remaining steps.

STEP 2. *READ THE SOCIAL COMPASS STORY.*

2a) Read "Alex Asks Questions."

Alex likes to talk. He especially loves to talk about the things he's interested in, such as bugs. At school, Alex talks to his classmates about his love for insects. Some of the boys like to listen to him tell them facts about bugs. One time, he started to tell a new student all about bugs. He was so busy talking that he didn't notice the new student was holding a grasshopper in a cage. When the boy realized that Alex was not going to ask him about his pet, the boy walked away. The boy was sad Alex wasn't interested in him and his grasshopper.

Alex was confused about why the boy left while he was still talking. But then he remembered something someone taught him once: Ask questions to find out why something is happening that you don't understand or know. Ask questions to let people know you like them and so they will want to keep talking to you. Alex pictured a Question Bubble in his head, which reminded him to ask questions. As the boy walked away, Alex looked at him and said, "Hey, why are you leaving?" The boy said he didn't think Alex wanted to talk to him. Alex did want to talk to him so he asked another question. He said, "Wait! Is that a grasshopper in that cage?" The boy was so happy that Alex noticed him and his grasshopper that he quickly came back over. He was interested in sharing his pet story with Alex. He liked that Alex asked him a question about himself.

Alex asked him why he brought a grasshopper to school. The boy told him it was his first day at school and he wanted to bring something to talk about with his new classmates. Alex understood that the boy liked grasshoppers as much as he liked bugs. They had a lot of information they could share about insects. They had a lot to find out about one another. Asking questions about people or what they are doing is a way to show people you care about them.

2b) Have the students answer comprehension questions.

The answers should resemble the following:

MODULE 4 READING COMPREHENSION SHEET

1. What was the visual support? Select one.

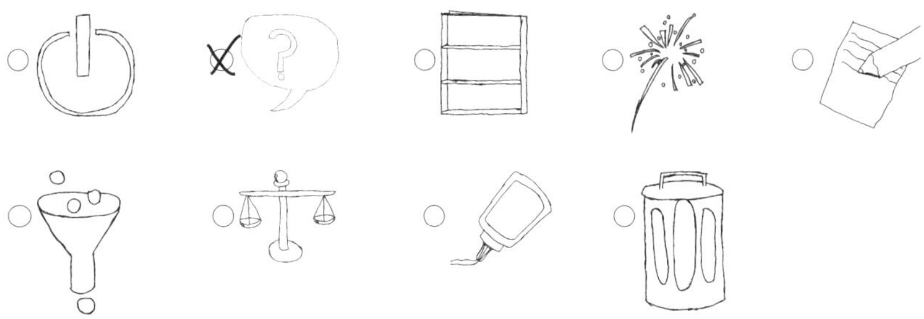

2. Who was the story about? Select one.
   - ○ Willy ○ Evan ○ Connie ⊗ Alex
   - ○ Sharon ○ Ned ○ Mike ○ Patrick ○ Frank

3. What was his or her problem? Select one.
   - ○ Didn't know how to compliment someone
   - ○ Didn't know when to stop talking
   - ○ Didn't share knowledge with others
   - ○ Didn't know how to start a conversation
   - ○ Didn't give friends a turn to talk
   - ○ Didn't know about things others know
   - ⊗ Didn't get more information
   - ○ Didn't think about what friends like
   - ○ Didn't seem to listen by checking in with the speaker

4. What did he or she learn to do about it? Write your answer.

   Alex learned that he needs to ask other people questions if he wants them to be interested in what he has to say and keep a conversation going.

5. Draw or summarize the story.

   Alex loved to talk about bugs to the other boys in his class, but he would not ask them questions about themselves. He realized that if he wants to talk about the things that interest him, he also needs to be interested in what the other kids have to say. He learned to express his interest by asking questions.

STEP 3. *MODEL AND REHEARSE.*

3a) Model asking questions during a conversation.

1. Place a large copy of the Question Bubble icon on the wall next to where you will be modeling asking questions.
2. Choose a student to come up and begin speaking to you.
3. Notice something about the student that you can ask a question about and say it out loud. For example, if your partner has on a new shirt, you could say out loud, "Hmmm, I've never seen Tom wear that shirt before. I'm going to ask him if it's new." Then, ask the question: "Tom, I like your shirt, is it new?"
4. After you model asking someone about noticeable information, pretend to recall information that is not readily noticeable but that you know about your conversation partner from previous interactions. Think out loud in order to demonstrate this idea. For example, say, "Yesterday when I saw Tom he said his computer broke; I am going to ask him if he fixed it." Then, ask the question: "Hey, Tom, have you fixed your computer yet?"

3b) Have the students rehearse asking questions during a conversation.

1. Ask for a volunteer to get up with you in front of the class. Have the student bring up a personal item (e.g., notebook, bag, book).
2. Begin a conversation with the student.
3. Periodically stop the conversation and ask the rest of the group to call out ideas for questions that you could ask your conversation partner. For example, "What's that book that you are holding?" Provide feedback to students and direct them to record their performance on Line A of the Self-Monitoring Data Sheet.
4. Then ask the audience to say things that they know about your conversation partner. For example, "He likes football," or "He has a younger sister."
5. Ask the audience to identify questions that are related to things that they have mentioned. For example, "When did you start playing football?"

3c) Prompt the students to record their data on Line B of the Self-Monitoring Data Sheet.

I can recall information about others to ask them a follow-up question

○ by myself ○ with peer help ○ with teacher help

STEP 4. *ROLE-PLAY AND REINFORCE.*

4a) Have students role-play asking questions during a conversation.

1. Place the students in pairs and provide them with conversation topics as needed.
2. Have the students practice asking each other questions during their conversation. The questions should be about information that is readily observable about a person and information that is previously known.
3. Provide feedback through verbal reinforcement when the student's questions are appropriate.
4. Have the students' peers provide feedback on the role play by giving them a "thumbs up" or "thumbs down."

4b) Prompt the students to mark their data on Line C of the Self-Monitoring Data Sheet.

I can role-play appropriate conversation questions with a partner

○ by myself ○ with peer help ○ with teacher help

STEP 5. *PROMOTE GENERALIZATION.*

Appendix B

Send home the Parent Follow-Up Page.

Follow-up directions are provided on the Parent Follow-Up Page.

LESSON 4C

SHARING INFORMATION

STEP 1. *EXPLAIN THE GOAL AND VISUAL SUPPORT.*

1a) Goal

The goal of this lesson is to teach students how to share their thoughts with others. Everyone's thoughts are unique and special. People share their thoughts with others so that they have something to speak about, they can get someone else's input, and oftentimes to even learn something about themselves. This helps people connect and learn more about each other.

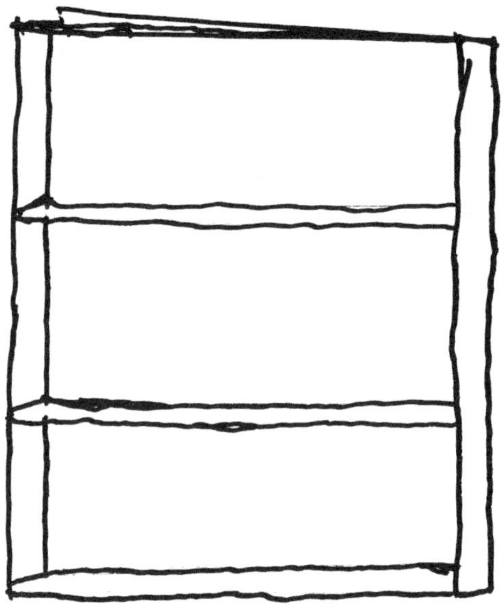

1b) Visual Support

The visual support for this lesson is a Display Case. An individual's thoughts are like a collection of prized belongings. Prized belongings are special. People share their prized belongings with others so that they can comment on them, admire them, and perhaps even add to an individual's knowledge about them.

Appendix A Appendix B

1c) Hand out Module 4, Lesson 4C Self-Monitoring Data Sheets to the students.

Provide all lesson handouts for the students to follow through with the remaining steps.

STEP 2. *READ THE SOCIAL COMPASS STORY.*

2a) Read "Sharon Shares Her Thoughts."

Sharon is very shy. She doesn't like to start conversations, and even when someone else starts, she doesn't like to continue. It is okay to be shy, but Sharon is unhappy that she has no close friends. She found the courage to ask a girl at school if she would go with her to a concert. The girl said no because she didn't really know Sharon that well.

Sharon was very upset by this rejection. She wanted to be closer to people, but she just didn't know what to say. She told her mom what the girl said to her. Her mom said that our minds are like display cases, which are cases that show special items that we have. In order to make friends, Sharon's mom said she should open up her thoughts and share them like she would share her special items in a display case. Sharon's mom said that for people to feel close to Sharon they need to know more about her. She needs to share her thoughts, ideas, and feelings with other people. So much of a conversation is about how someone feels and thinks. So Sharon set off to start sharing.

The next day at school, she sat near a group of girls she knew. They began to talk about a movie. Sharon stepped closer and waited to speak. As the girls saw she had something to say, they stopped and listened. She said she thought the movie was very good and she would like to see another movie. Just then, another girl said she wanted to see the same movie. She asked Sharon if she would like to go with her on the weekend. Sharon was so excited that she said yes right away. Opening up with her thoughts also opened up a chance to make a friend.

2b. Have the students answer comprehension questions.

The answers should resemble the following:

MODULE 4 READING COMPREHENSION SHEET

1. What was the visual support? Select one.

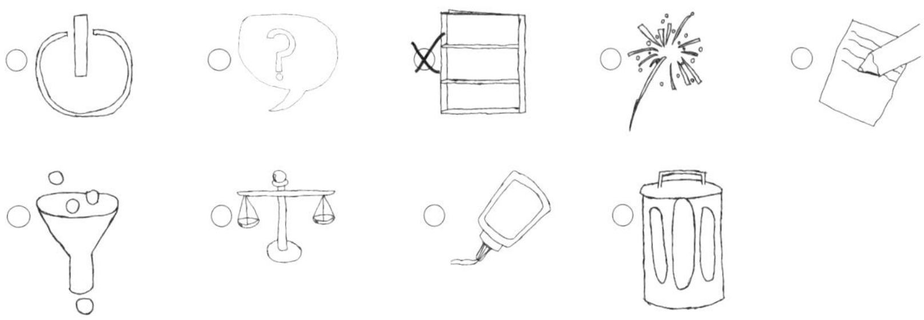

2. Who was the story about? Select one.

○ Willy ○ Evan ○ Connie ○ Alex
☒ Sharon ○ Ned ○ Mike ○ Patrick ○ Frank

3. What was his or her problem? Select one.
   - ○ Didn't know how to compliment someone
   - ○ Didn't know when to stop talking
   - ☒ Didn't share knowledge with others
   - ○ Didn't know how to start a conversation
   - ○ Didn't give friends a turn to talk
   - ○ Didn't know about things others know
   - ○ Didn't get more information
   - ○ Didn't think about what friends like
   - ○ Didn't seem to listen by checking in with the speaker

4. What did he or she learn to do about it? Write your answer.

   Sharon learned to share her thoughts and opinions so that she could join in the conversations around her.

5. Draw or summarize the story.

   Sharon was shy, but she learned to open up and share her interests. She made a friend.

STEP 3. *MODEL AND REHEARSE.*

3a) Model sharing information.

1. Refer students to the list of interests on the Interest Inventory handout (found in Appendix B and among the accompanying online materials) and mark Line A on their Self-Monitoring Data Sheets.
2. Complete the inventory out loud, and encourage the students to complete their list along with you on their Self-Monitoring Data Sheets.
3. Have the students choose partners and practice sharing their interests by reading their lists to one another. (If a student needs additional help, have the previous lesson with the Start Button visual available for cuing or prompting as well.)

3b) Have the students rehearse sharing information.

1. In a group, have the students talk with each other to learn about their peers' interests.
2. After a short time, place the students in pairs.
3. Have the students in each pair interview one another to find out what they like and fill out the Interest Inventory handout with their partner's interests.
4. Prompt the students to then engage in a short conversation about one interest on their data sheets.

3c) Prompt the students to mark Line B on the Self-Monitoring Data Sheet.

I can generate a unique piece of personal information to share

○ by myself ○ with peer help ○ with teacher help

STEP 4. *ROLE-PLAY AND REINFORCE.*

4a) Have the students role-play sharing information.

1. Refer students to the Display Case visual support.
2. Have the students spend a few minutes either writing or drawing their own interests on the handout.
3. Place the students in pairs and have them interview each other by asking, "What do you like to do?" Students can refer to their Display Cases as a reminder to open up and share their interests.
4. Have partners respond with a related follow-up question about the other student's interests.
5. Reinforce and provide feedback.

4b) Prompt the students to mark Line C of the Self-Monitoring Data Sheet.

I can role play sharing information about myself in a conversation with a peer

○ by myself ○ with peer help ○ with teacher help

STEP 5. *PROMOTE GENERALIZATION.*

Appendix B

Send home the Parent Follow-Up Page.

Follow-up directions are provided on the Parent Follow-Up Page.

LESSON 4D
GIVING COMPLIMENTS

STEP 1. *EXPLAIN THE GOAL AND VISUAL SUPPORT.*

1a) Goal

The goal of this lesson is to help students understand the importance of complimenting others. Complimenting communicates a positive thought to another person, which often results in positive thoughts about you. Complimenting someone is also another way to start a conversation.

1b) Visual Support

People often use confetti when throwing parties to add color and joy to an event. When people see confetti, it can make them happy and feel good. In a conversation, a compliment can add some color and joy to your conversation. This lesson uses the Compliment Confetti icon to remind students of the joy of giving and getting compliments.

1c) Hand out Module 4, Lesson 4D Self-Monitoring Data Sheets to the students.

Appendix A Appendix B

Provide all lesson handouts for the students to follow through with the remaining steps.

STEP 2. *READ THE SOCIAL COMPASS STORY.*

2a) Read "Connie Compliments."

Connie is a new student. She wants to meet some girls to sit with at lunch. At morning recess, she walked up to some girls and announced that she has a new pet at home. The other girls were confused and did not understand why Connie would share that with them, so they walked away from her. Connie was sad. An older student saw what happened and suggested that Connie try another strategy to get their attention and try to make friends. She suggested that Connie begin a conversation with people she wants to get to know with a compliment. A compliment is a statement about the nice aspects of someone, such as the way they look or something great they did. The student said that Connie could try to imagine throwing a handful of Compliment Confetti at a party to remember to compliment someone.

When it was time for Connie to get in the lunch line, she said to a girl in her new class, "Oh wow, I like your book bag." This was a sincere statement, and the girl could tell that Connie was making an effort to be nice. This made the girl happy and interested in getting to know Connie. The girl thanked Connie and asked if she was a new student. Connie told her it was her first day and she didn't even know yet where she was supposed to sit at lunch. The girl invited Connie to sit with her. This made Connie happy.

2b) Have the students answer comprehension questions.
The answers should resemble the following:

MODULE 4 READING COMPREHENSION SHEET

1. What was the visual support? Select one.

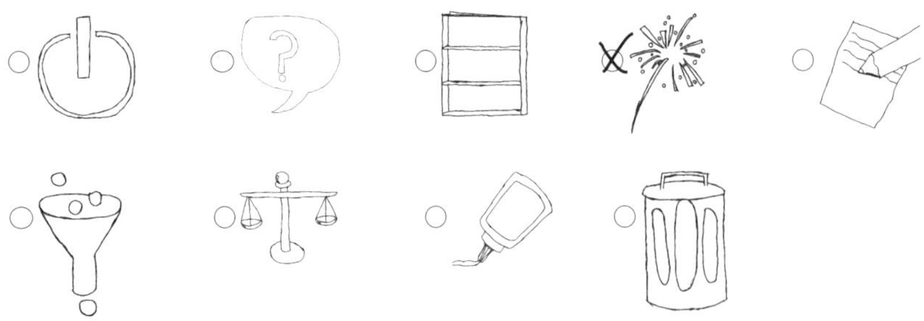

2. Who was the story about? Select one.
○ Willy ○ Evan ☒ Connie ○ Alex
○ Sharon ○ Ned ○ Mike ○ Patrick ○ Frank

3. What was his or her problem? Select one.
   - ☒ Didn't know how to compliment someone
   - ○ Didn't know when to stop talking
   - ○ Didn't share knowledge with others
   - ○ Didn't know how to start a conversation
   - ○ Didn't give friends a turn to talk
   - ○ Didn't know about things others know
   - ○ Didn't get more information
   - ○ Didn't think about what friends like
   - ○ Didn't seem to listen by checking in with the speaker

4. What did he or she learn to do about it? Write your answer.

   Connie was a new girl at school and did not have any friends. She learned that she could start conversations and even make friends by complimenting others.

5. Draw or summarize the story.

   Connie had not made friends. She complimented a girl's backpack, they started talking, and then they became friends.

STEP 3. *MODEL AND REHEARSE.*

3a) Model giving compliments.

Demonstrate complimenting to the students by walking around the room and giving each student a genuine compliment. Ask students why giving compliments is important. Provide feedback for each response. Prompt students to mark their data on Line A of the Self-Monitoring Data Sheet.

3b) Have the students rehearse giving compliments.

As a whole group play "Compliment Hot Potato":

1. Have everyone sit in a circle.
2. Refer students to the Compliment Confetti visual support.
3. Pass an object around the circle, and have each student give a compliment to the person he or she is passing the object to.
4. If a student is unable to give a compliment, provide some prompts to encourage him or her.

3c) Prompt the students to mark their data on Line B on the Self-Monitoring Data Sheet.

I can generate compliments in structured play

○ by myself ○ with peer help ○ with teacher help

STEP 4. *ROLE-PLAY AND REINFORCE.*

4a) Have the students role-play giving compliments.

1. Place the students in pairs.
2. Have each pair get up in front of the group, and have each student in the pair compliment the other student. (Prompt as needed.)
3. Provide feedback as a group.

4b) Prompt the students to mark Line C of the Self-Monitoring Data Sheet.

I can role-play giving and receiving compliments in a conversation with a partner

○ by myself ○ with peer help ○ with teacher help

STEP 5. *PROMOTE GENERALIZATION.*

Appendix B

Send home the Parent Follow-Up Page.

Follow-up directions are provided on the Parent Follow-Up Page.

LESSON 4E

EXPANDING PERSONAL INTERESTS

STEP 1. *EXPLAIN THE GOAL AND VISUAL SUPPORT.*

1a) Goal

The goal of this lesson is to teach students how to become more engaged and more knowledgeable about the world and people in it. The more interests an individual has, the easier it may be to participate in activities and conversations. People can always add new interests to their personal interest inventory.

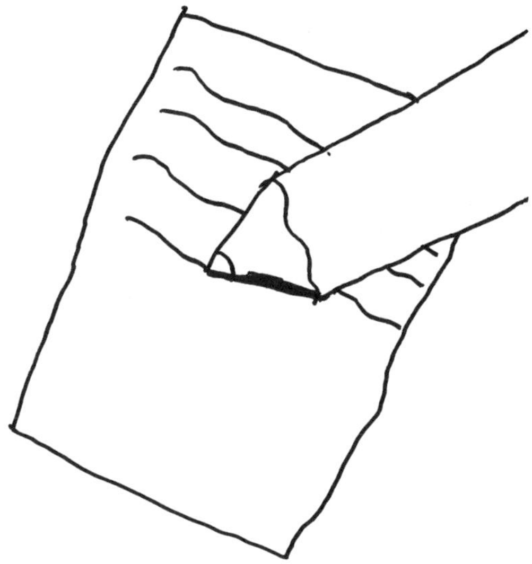

1b) Visual Support

An inventory list keeps track of what you have. The visual support for this lesson is the Interest Inventory checklist from Lesson 4C. This list of potential new interests helps remind students that they can add to their current knowledge and interests at any time.

Appendix A Appendix B

1c) Hand out Module 4, Lesson 4E Self-Monitoring Data Sheets to the students.

Provide all lesson handouts for the students to follow through with the remaining steps.

STEP 2. *READ THE SOCIAL COMPASS STORY.*

2a) Read "Evan's Endless Interests."

Evan is fun to talk to. He knows so much about so many things. He can talk for several hours without repeating topics. Evan's friends learn so much from listening to him. And he learns so much from being a good listener, too. It all began when Evan was small. He listened really carefully to his grandpa when he talked. Evan asked questions about when his grandpa was a small boy. Evan thought talking with his grandpa was fascinating. Some of his grandpa's interests were airplanes, trucks, animals, and gardening. Evan became interested in some of these things, too. He reviewed his Interest Inventory in his head. He didn't know much about some of his grandpa's interests, so he made a mental note to add them to his list of possible interests.

Evan also liked talking with his cousins and Aunt Lu. His aunt told them stories about dancing, making cookies, and old-fashioned clothes. Evan realized that people's brains are like computers and they can store information and update their interests, just like they update their computers. People's different interests make life more interesting. When he listened to what people around him were sharing, his own interests grew and grew and grew. Now he always has something interesting to say. If he doesn't have something to add to a conversation, he listens carefully and still takes an interest in the conversation.

2b) Have the students answer comprehension questions.

The answers should resemble the following:

MODULE 4 READING COMPREHENSION SHEET

1. What was the visual support? Select one.

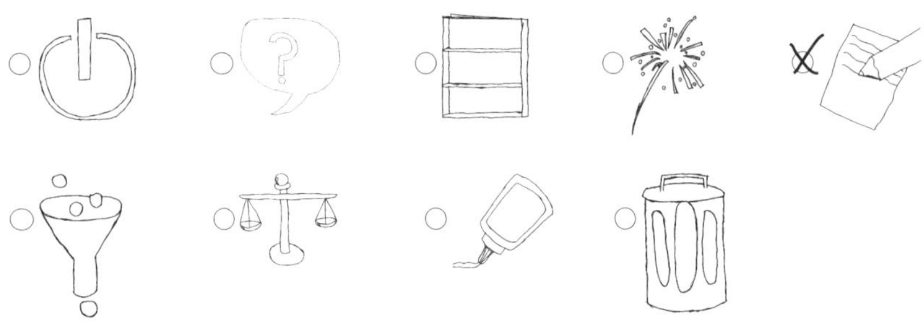

2. Who was the story about? Select one.

○ Willy ☒ Evan ○ Connie ○ Alex
○ Sharon ○ Ned ○ Mike ○ Patrick ○ Frank

3. What was his or her problem? Select one.

○ Didn't know how to compliment someone
○ Didn't know when to stop talking
○ Didn't share knowledge with others
○ Didn't know how to start a conversation
○ Didn't give friends a turn to talk
☒ Didn't know about things others know
○ Didn't get more information
○ Didn't think about what friends like
○ Didn't seem to listen by checking in with the speaker

4. What did he or she learn to do about it? Write your answer.

   Evan realized that learning more about things other people are interested in can result in being interested in more things yourself.

5. Draw or summarize the story.

   Evan listened to everyone around him and learned to talk to others about new and interesting things.

STEP 3. MODEL AND REHEARSE.

3a) Model using the Interest Inventory.

Read the Interest Inventory aloud to the class and check off your interests.

3b) Have the students rehearse using the Interest Inventory.

1. Give the students a few minutes to recall five of their interests from their Interest Inventory and record their data on Line A of their Self-Monitoring Data Sheets.
2. Have the students identify a possible new interest for themselves from the list of your interests.
3. Provide praise for correct answers, and prompt students who do not respond by showing them your copy of the inventory.

3c) Prompt the students to mark Line B on the Self-Monitoring Data Sheet.

I can identify a possible new interest that the teacher has that is different from any of my interests

◯ by myself ◯ with peer help ◯ with teacher help

STEP 4. *ROLE-PLAY AND REINFORCE.*

4a) Have the students role-play sharing interests.

1. Place the students in pairs, and have them engage in conversations about their personal interests as they go through the Interest Inventory. You can prompt the students to interview each other to see if they are interested in the same things.
2. If is the students identify a shared interest, prompt them to extend the questions to ask more about this interest.
3. Have the students in each pair go through the whole inventory and count up how many interests they share.
4. Have the students discuss a new interest they may develop from this interaction.

4b) Prompt the students to mark their data on Line C of the Self-Monitoring Data Sheet.

I can identify a possible new interest from my interaction with someone in the group

◯ by myself ◯ with peer help ◯ with teacher help

STEP 5. *PROMOTE GENERALIZATION.*

Appendix B

Send home the Parent Follow-Up Page.

Follow-up directions are provided on the Parent Follow-Up Page.

LESSON 4F

PARAPHRASING

STEP 1. *EXPLAIN THE GOAL AND VISUAL SUPPORT.*

1a) Goal

The goal of this lesson is to have the students learn how to demonstrate active listening during a conversation so that they can paraphrase, or repeat back in a condensed way, what the other person was saying. This shows a conversation partner that the other person has been listening to what he or she has to say.

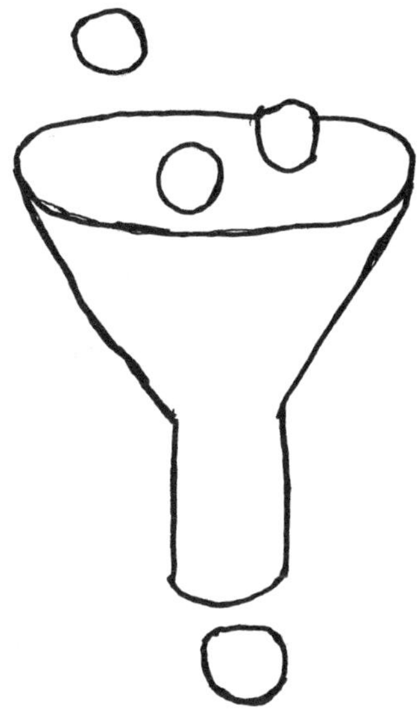

1b) Visual Support

A funnel takes liquid in from a large opening and ciphers it down into a small opening. The art of paraphrasing requires someone to take a whole conversation and shrink it down into a short summary. The visual support for this lesson is a Paraphrasing Funnel, which helps the students understand how to take a big idea and fit it in a smaller conversation.

1c) Hand out Module 4, Lesson 4F Self-Monitoring Data Sheets to the students.

Provide all lesson handouts for the students to follow through with the remaining steps.

STEP 2. *READ THE SOCIAL COMPASS STORY.*

2a) Read "Patrick's Paraphrase."

At school Patrick talks to his friends. He likes to talk about sports, but some of his friends don't like sports. His friend George sometimes loses interest when he talks with Patrick. George gets bored listening to Patrick talk about sports. George feels that Patrick doesn't even hear a thing that he says in their conversations. In fact, one day George purposefully listened to see if Patrick was paying any attention to George's comments.

He walked up and asked if George saw the basketball game last night. George said no and that he was not feeling well. Patrick said it was a very good game, too bad he missed it. George said he was so sick last night he threw up. Patrick said the score was very close until the end. Just then, George knew that Patrick was not actively listening

to him. George told Patrick he didn't want to talk with him anymore if Patrick couldn't learn to listen to what he had to say. Patrick was confused. He asked George to explain how he could talk to someone and listen to them in the same conversation. George said that you need to check in with each other when you talk. Sometimes you talk and sometimes you listen and condense what the other person says. This shows the other person that you understand what they are saying, and if you happen to not understand, this is the time you can try again to understand. George said to imagine a Paraphrasing Funnel with words pouring into the listener's ears and only the few most important words coming back out of the listener's mouth.

Patrick thought this was a good idea and tried it the next day. When he saw George, he said, "Hi, did you see the game last night?" George said, "No, I was really sick," and he went on to tell him in detail all about the horrible evening he had the night before. Patrick said, "You are still sick; it has been a few days now, right?" George laughed and said, "No, I am not really sick, I was just seeing if you were listening to me." Both the boys laughed and felt good. Understanding the importance of listening and paraphrasing saved their friendship from ending.

2b) Have the students answer comprehension questions.

The answers should resemble the following:

MODULE 4 READING COMPREHENSION SHEET

1. What was the visual support? Select one.

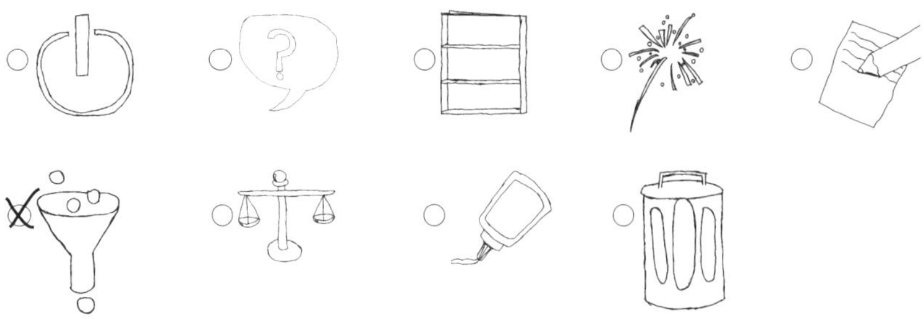

2. Who was the story about? Select one.

○ Willy ○ Evan ○ Connie ○ Alex
○ Sharon ○ Ned ○ Mike ☒ Patrick ○ Frank

3. What was his or her problem? Select one.
   - ◯ Didn't know how to compliment someone
   - ◯ Didn't know when to stop talking
   - ◯ Didn't share knowledge with others
   - ◯ Didn't know how to start a conversation
   - ◯ Didn't give friends a turn to talk
   - ◯ Didn't know about things others know
   - ◯ Didn't get more information
   - ◯ Didn't think about what friends like
   - ☒ Didn't seem to listen by checking in with the speaker

4. What did he or she learn to do about it? Write your answer.

   Patrick learned to repeat back something he heard to confirm he was listening carefully to his friend.

5. Draw or summarize the story.

   Patrick doesn't listen to his friend. His friend gets mad. Patrick learns to pay closer attention and paraphrase what his friend says, and it fixes their friendship.

STEP 3. *MODEL AND REHEARSE.*

3a) Model good listening and paraphrasing.

1. Tell the class in several detailed sentences about your experience in a grocery store. Provide a narrative of a typical trip, and describe it in full detail for about a minute.
2. Have the students identify the key components of your story that would best describe a condensed version, as if the words had been pushed through a funnel and only the relevant words or new words that summarize come out of the funnel. Provide feedback for each response shared with the group. Refer students to the Paraphrasing Funnel icon and point to where each of their responses would fit in a funnel. Would it get stuck at the top, or is it meaningful enough to make its way through to the end? Have students mark their data on Line A of the Self-Monitoring Data Sheet.
3. Do the entire exercise again, but this time tell the students what happened in a TV show you saw the night before and have the group paraphrase back, "Your show was about…." (You may need to do this a couple of times so that the students really see how to do this.)

3b) Have the students rehearse good listening and paraphrasing.

Rehearse paraphrasing by playing pronoun Simon Says as a group. You say "I went to the store and saw you there." Have the students respond together by saying, "You went to the store and saw me there." Add more sentences, but limit their responses to one sentence.

3c) Prompt the students to mark their data on Line B of the Self-Monitoring Data Sheet.

I can paraphrase with a correct pronoun in a structured game of Simon Says

○ by myself ○ with peer help ○ with teacher help

STEP 4. *ROLE-PLAY AND REINFORCE.*

4a) Have the students role-play paraphrasing.

1. Place the students in pairs, and have each pair role-play for the rest of the class.
2. In each pair, have one student tell the other student about a book he or she read, a game he or she played, or somewhere he or she visited. Have the other student paraphrase what he or she heard.
3. The group should give a "thumbs up" when they hear someone paraphrasing correctly.
4. Provide feedback to each student

4b) Prompt the students to mark their data on Line C of the Self-Monitoring Data Sheet.

I can paraphrase in a conversation with a partner

○ by myself ○ with peer help ○ with teacher help

STEP 5. *PROMOTE GENERALIZATION.*

Appendix B

Send home the Parent Follow-Up Page.

Follow-up directions are provided on the Parent Follow-Up Page.

LESSON 4G

NEGOTIATING NEEDS

STEP 1. *EXPLAIN THE GOAL AND VISUAL SUPPORT.*

1a) Goal.

The goal of this lesson is for students to learn how to be a good friend by balancing their wants with a friend's wants. Ideally, a relationship looks like a scale that is perfectly balanced, in which the needs and wants of each person are equally important.

1b) Visual Support

A scale is a tool to weigh items. A balance is often depicted as having two sides to weigh against one another. The Friendship Balance is a visual reminder that students need to weigh their needs with the needs of their friends to come up with a balance that makes them both happy. The scale shows the focus that is placed on each person's interest and not on one over the other's.

Appendix A Appendix B

1c) Hand out Module 4, Lesson 4G Self-Monitoring Data Sheets to the students.

Provide all lesson handouts for the students to follow through with the remaining steps.

STEP 2. *READ THE SOCIAL COMPASS STORY.*

2a) Read "Frank Finds the Balance."

Finding a friend is not always easy. And being a fine friend like Frank is even harder. Frank is a special friend because he is good at sharing. He shares his snacks at lunch, he shares his books, and he shares stories about himself. Sharing things with Frank is fun, most of the time.

One time, for a whole week of school, Frank went on the computer first every day. His friends got upset with him and told him that they did not want to be friends with him anymore. Frank thought this was great at first, but the other kids thought that he was being selfish and that he was not thinking about how they were feeling. This was not how Frank wanted his friends to think about him.

Frank was sad and talked with his mom about his problem. She told him he needed to learn to negotiate. This meant that he could compromise or decide on a plan that isn't exactly what he wanted because he is more interested in the friendship than his own interests.

Now, to decide how to negotiate a situation, Frank pictures a Friendship Balance. He weighs his options by thinking about a balancing scale; something can tip to one side if it is not even or balanced. He wants to keep the scale balanced by putting equal amounts on both sides. If Frank always gets everything his way, the scale will not be balanced. It will be tipped to Frank's side. At first Frank may be happy, but Frank knows that if he always gets what he wants, others may be unhappy, which might make them not want to be his friends.

So, Frank thought of his friendship balance. How can he keep both sides equal? He decides he can let a friend go first on the computer sometimes. Getting to be first on the computer makes his friend smile. Frank and his friend will each get a chance to be first...one time it may be Frank's turn, and the next time it may be his friend's turn. Now there is a balance. Now Frank is smiling. Negotiating is a smart thing to do to keep friends happy.

2b) Have the students answer comprehension questions.

The answers should resemble the following:

MODULE 4 READING COMPREHENSION SHEET

1. What was the visual support? Select one.

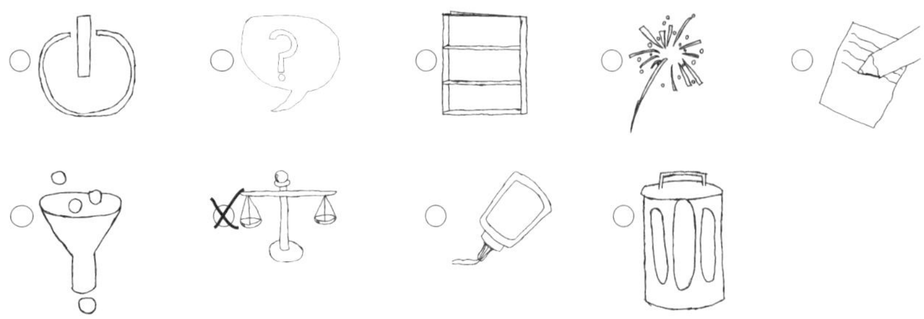

2. Who was the story about? Select one.

○ Willy ○ Evan ○ Connie ○ Alex
○ Sharon ○ Ned ○ Mike ○ Patrick ☒ Frank

3. What was his or her problem? Select one.
   ○ Didn't know how to compliment someone
   ○ Didn't know when to stop talking
   ○ Didn't share knowledge with others
   ○ Didn't know how to start a conversation
   ○ Didn't give friends a turn to talk
   ○ Didn't know about things others know
   ○ Didn't get more information
   ☒ Didn't think about what friends like
   ○ Didn't seem to listen by checking in with the speaker

4. What did he or she learn to do about it? Write your answer.

   Frank learned to balance his friend's needs with his own. He realized he could share the chance to take the first turn on the computer and everyone would be happy.

5. Draw or summarize the story.

   Frank wants to make his friends happy and keep them happy, so he takes turns and compromises with them.

STEP 3. *MODEL AND REHEARSE.*

3a) Model maintaining balance in a group conversation:

Model for the students how to maintain balance when there are various interests at play.

1. Ask the class what game they'd like to play. It is highly likely that you'll get numerous different suggestions.
2. Refer the students to the Friendship Balance visual support. Review the various suggestions the students give, and tell them that they need to narrow down the choices.
3. Hold your hands up to signify a balance and say, "To keep things balanced, how about we play this game for a bit, then we'll play this other game?" Or you could say that you'll play one game today, the next game tomorrow, and so forth. Explain that this compromise will satisfy everyone's requests.

3b) Have the students rehearse maintaining balance.

Have the students raise their hands to provide a solution to the following modeled conversation. Ask the class, "What game do you want to play?" Call on a student to provide an answer. Once that student states a game, call on another student and ask, "What game do you want to play?" Call on a third student and ask, "What game do you want to play?" Then ask the class, "If we only have 15 minutes to play, how could we proceed in a balanced way?" The students should raise hands to provide a solution.

3c) Prompt the students to mark their data on Line A of the Self-Monitoring Data Sheet.

I can suggest a way to balance the group's choice

○ by myself ○ with peer help ○ with teacher help

STEP 4. *ROLE-PLAY AND REINFORCE.*

4a) Have the students role-play maintaining balance when trying to agree on something.

1. Place the students in pairs, and have them role-play having a conversation about making plans to do something together after school.
2. Ensure the students take turns expressing their interests and listening to their partner's interests.
3. Have the students decide together how they will balance each partner's needs.
4. After they have had some time to practice their conversation on their own, have each pair role-play their conversation in front of the whole group.
5. Ask the group to label how members of the pair balanced their needs: Did they compromise? Did they negotiate so that one person's needs will be met this time and the other person's needs will be met at another time? Have students give a "thumbs up" or "thumbs down" to indicate if the pair found a balance. Provide feedback.
6. Provide prompts to assist when students don't demonstrate the targeted skills.

4b) Prompt the students to mark their data on Line B of the Self-Monitoring Data Sheet.

I can role-play negotiating my wants with another person's wants

○ by myself ○ with peer help ○ with teacher help

STEP 5. *PROMOTE GENERALIZATION.*

Appendix B

Send home the Parent Follow-Up Page.

Follow-up directions are provided on the Parent Follow-Up Page.

LESSON 4H
MAINTAINING A CONVERSATION

STEP 1. *EXPLAIN THE GOAL AND VISUAL SUPPORT.*

1a) Goal

The goal of this lesson is to teach students how to maintain a conversation in an effective manner. Sticking to the main point of the conversation and being an interested, engaged listener helps to keep a conversation going.

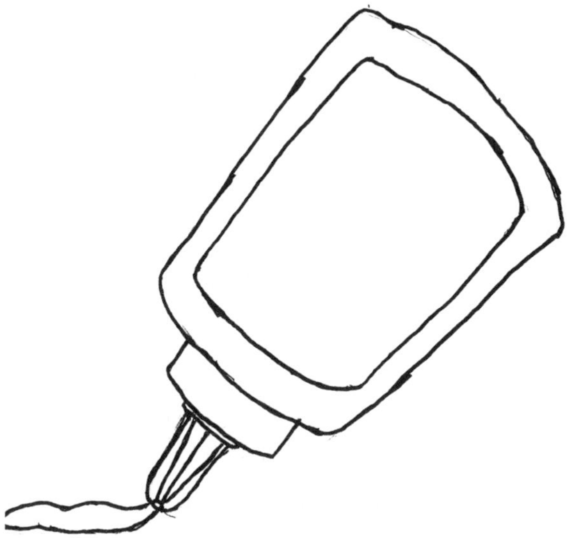

1b) Visual Support

Glue holds objects together. The Conversation Glue visual support illustrates the concept of using relevant words as an adhesive to hold a conversation together.

Appendix A Appendix B

1c) Hand out Module 4, Lesson 4H Self-Monitoring Data Sheets to the students.

Provide all lesson handouts for the students to follow through with the remaining steps.

STEP 2. *READ THE SOCIAL COMPASS STORY.*

2a) Read "Mike Maintains a Conversation."

Mike knows how to begin a conversation, but when it comes to maintaining one, he crashes. Sometimes he talks like the conversation is just for him; he doesn't give the person he is speaking with a chance to speak. This is called talking AT someone rather than talking WITH someone. In order to talk with someone, Mike needs to use his Conversation Glue and take turns with the person he is speaking with to hold his conversations together. Some different types of Conversation Glue that Mike can try include

Taking turns: Make a few statements and then stop to let the other person make a few statements while you listen.

Repeating: Every so often, repeat back parts of what the other person says.

Nodding: Nod to show agreement or understanding of what the other person says.

Commenting: Add your feedback about what is being said.

These strategies hold the conversation together like glue. Each person's sentences are joined to the other's. This is an example of what a conversation looks like when it is glued together:

Ned: "Hi Mike, how was your weekend?"

Mike: "Hey Ned, it was great." (He gave an answer related to Ned's question.) "How was your weekend Ned?" (He asked a question that was similar to the one he just answered.)

Ned: "Oh it was terrible!"

Mike: "Oh, that is too bad. Why was it terrible?" (He commented with his feedback and asked for more information.)

Ned: "Because I lost my homework."

Mike knew having a conversation meant keeping the conversation glued together by staying on topic and allowing the other person to speak. Mike stayed with the topic. He heard the emotion word "terrible" and decided to show Ned he was concerned by asking more questions.

Active listening and asking questions are two ways Mike can maintain a conversation. Mike likes that he can support his friend by maintaining a conversation using his Conversation Glue. Ned likes this too!

2b) Have the students answer comprehension questions.

The answers should resemble the following:

MODULE 4 READING COMPREHENSION SHEET

1. What was the visual support? Select one.

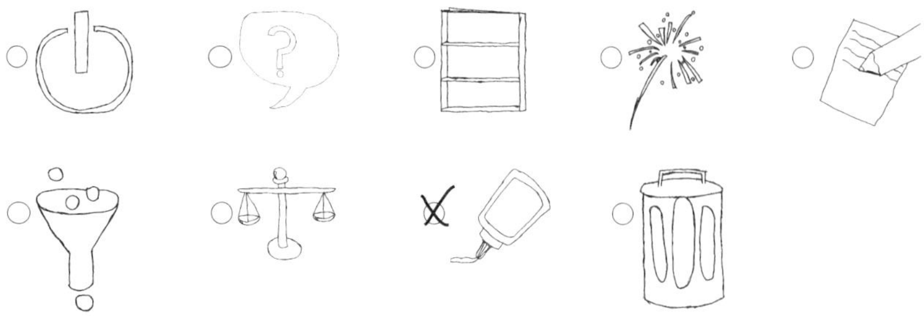

2. Who was the story about? Select one.

○ Willy ○ Evan ○ Connie ○ Alex
○ Sharon ○ Ned ☒ Mike ○ Patrick ○ Frank

3. What was his or her problem? Select one.
   - ○ Didn't know how to compliment someone
   - ○ Didn't know when to stop talking
   - ○ Didn't share knowledge with others
   - ○ Didn't know how to start a conversation
   - ☒ Didn't give friends a turn to talk
   - ○ Didn't know about things others know
   - ○ Didn't get more information
   - ○ Didn't think about what friends like
   - ○ Didn't seem to listen by checking in with the speaker

4. What did he or she learn to do about it? Write your answer.

   Mike learned that there are a few strategies to use to hold a conversation together: take turns, be a good listener, look at the speaker, repeat, nod, and comment.

5. Draw or summarize the story.

   Mike had a hard time keeping conversations together until he learned the strategies to help him maintain them.

STEP 3. MODEL AND REHEARSE.

3a) Model maintaining a conversation.

Demonstrate each of these strategies mentioned in "Mike Maintains a Conversation."

Taking turns: Make a few statements and then stop to let the other person make a few statements while you listen.

Repeating: Every so often, repeat back parts of what the other person says.

Nodding: This shows agreement or understanding of what the other person says.

Commenting: Add your feedback about what is being said to participate in the conversation.

3b) Have the students rehearse maintaining a conversation.

1. Ask the students what the Conversation Glue visual support represents. The answer should be that it includes strategies (e.g., taking turns, repeating back part of what the other person says, commenting) to help maintain a conversation and hold it together.
2. Ask for two volunteers to demonstrate each of the strategies discussed in "Mike Maintains a Conversation": taking turns, repeating, nodding, and commenting. Provide feedback and prompts as needed. Have the volunteers select the strategy privately so students need to pay attention and discriminate which strategy is being modeled. Instruct the observing students to raise their hands when they see the target skill.

Prompt the observing students to mark their data on Line A of the Self-Monitoring Data Sheet.

I can identify behaviors in a model that keep a conversation going

○ by myself ○ with peer help ○ with teacher help

3c) Have all of the students rehearse maintaining a conversation.

1. Place the students in pairs and have them rehearse each Conversation Glue strategy one by one. Announce the first strategy and invite the pairs to begin. Give 1 minute of time and announce the next strategy to practice; repeat until the list is complete.
2. Each student should rehearse each strategy at least once.
3. Provide conversation topics if needed. Examples include current movies, video games, and homework. Provide feedback.

3d) Prompt the students to mark their data on Line B of the Self-Monitoring Data Sheet.

STEP 4. *ROLE-PLAY AND REINFORCE.*

4a) Have the students role-play maintaining a conversation.

After the pairs rehearse on their own, give each pair a chance to role-play their conversation in front of the group. Have the group provide each pair with a "thumbs up" each time one of the students uses a Conversation Glue strategy.

4b) Prompt the students to mark their data on Line C of the Self-Monitoring Data Sheet.

I can maintain a conversation in role play

○ by myself ○ with peer help ○ with teacher help

STEP 5. *PROMOTE GENERALIZATION.*

Appendix B

Send home the Parent Follow-Up Page.

Follow-up directions are provided on the Parent Follow-Up Page.

LESSON 41

ENDING A CONVERSATION

STEP 1. *EXPLAIN THE GOAL AND VISUAL SUPPORT.*

1a) Goal

The goal of this lesson is to have students practice ending conversations gracefully and naturally. Although conversations can be really enjoyable, it is important to know how to end them and move on.

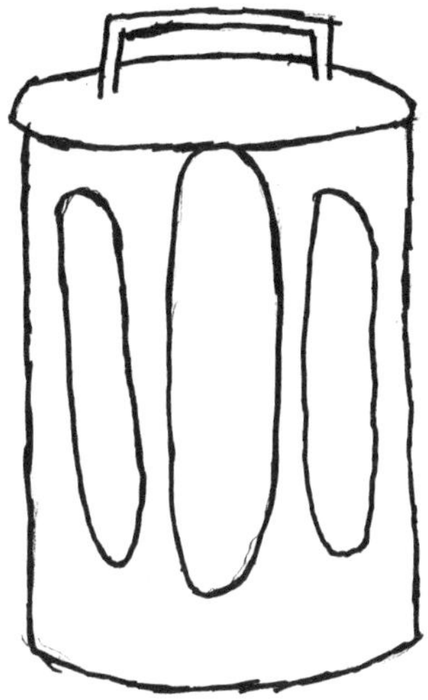

1b) Visual Support

A trash can holds waste. Just like you need to wrap up your trash and throw it in the can when you finish eating your lunch, for example, you need to clean up all of the loose ends and put them away when a conversation is over. The visual support for this lesson, therefore, is a Time's-Up Tin. The Time's-Up Tin will help students visualize ending a conversation by wrapping it up and putting it in the trash.

Appendix A Appendix B

1c) Hand out Module 4, Lesson 41 data sheets to the students.

Provide all lesson handouts for the students to follow through with the remaining steps.

STEP 2. *READ THE SOCIAL COMPASS STORY.*

2a) Read "Willy Wraps It Up."

Willy loves school. He loves science class. In science class he gets to bring in projects to share with the class. He gets to be in the spotlight for 5 minutes every Friday. He loves to talk about his projects.

Part of the spotlight time in science class includes a time for questions. Willy is good at talking. Sometimes he gives too much information. Too many details make people lose interest. He does not look at others to see if they are still interested or even paying attention. One time in school, he brought in his model of a rocket ship for spotlight time. He explained how it worked and where he bought the materials. He explained everything he could think of about his rocket ship. He did such a good job explaining his model that no one had any questions. So he decided to keep talking.

When he looked at his classmates to see if they were still listening, they all had put their heads on their desks. He was afraid they might have even fallen asleep. "How could this happen?" thought Willy. Rockets were fascinating to him and he had more information that he could say about them. When his time was up, his teacher said, "Thank you, Willy," and Willy sat down. He sat in his chair and thought about why no one was listening to him. He was a little angry that everyone ignored him at the end.

Next, it was Sally's spotlight time. She spoke and answered questions. She was thinking about what her classmates were thinking as she spoke. When she began a long sentence, she paused and looked at her classmates; if everyone was looking, she finished her sentence. If most people were not looking at her, she changed how she was explaining her project.

Willy noticed that Sally used the following strategies:

—Thinking about the listeners

—Thinking about how to keep the listeners interested

—Thinking about what to do when the listeners are finished listening

Willy asked his teacher what he could do to end his presentation instead of just being told to stop. His teacher said that Willy should pay attention to the people who are listening to him and learn to "wrap it up and throw it away" while people are still interested in what he is saying. She pointed to the trash can and told him to think of his own Time's-Up Tin as a visual reminder to end a conversation. Willy laughed at his teacher's words. He knew his teacher was telling him in a gentle way to learn about how to end a presentation.

The next week, Willy focused on his ending. He looked at his classmates as he spoke. He slowed down and paused when they looked away. He waited for them to look at him before he started again. He looked to see how much time he had. He had 1 minute to go. He asked if anyone had any questions. No one had any questions, so he said to himself, "Wrap it up and throw it away." He ended his presentation with a sentence he had practiced before the presentation. He said, "That is all for today." Everybody, including the teacher, smiled and clapped. Willy was proud of his ability to "wrap it up and throw it away."

2b) Have the students answer comprehension questions.

The answers should resemble the following:

MODULE 4 READING COMPREHENSION SHEET

1. What was the visual support? Select one.

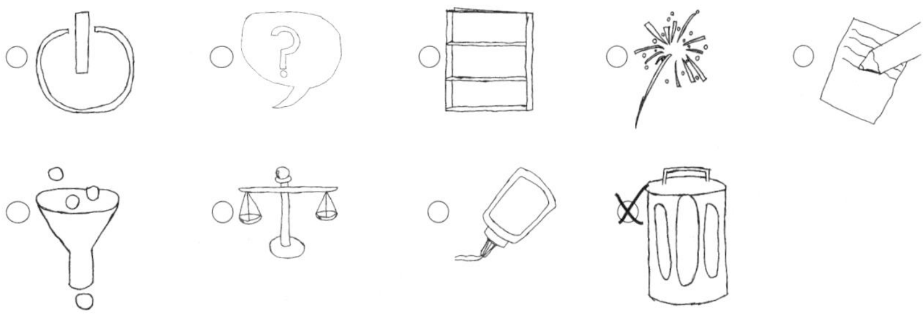

2. Who was the story about? Select one.

☒ Willy ○ Evan ○ Connie ○ Alex
○ Sharon ○ Ned ○ Mike ○ Patrick ○ Frank

3. What was his or her problem? Select one.

○ Didn't know how to compliment someone
☒ Didn't know when to stop talking
○ Didn't share knowledge with others
○ Didn't know how to start a conversation
○ Didn't give friends a turn to talk
○ Didn't know about things others know
○ Didn't get more information
○ Didn't think about what friends like
○ Didn't seem to listen by checking in with the speaker

4. What did he or she learn to do about it? Write your answer.

Willy learned to pay more attention to his listeners so that he can wrap up his thoughts and stop talking before they lose interest.

5. Draw or summarize the story.

Willy loves to talk. Sometimes when he is talking he doesn't stop, and people get bored with him. This happened at school, and he learned to look at other people to see when it was time to wrap up a conversation and throw it away.

STEP 3. *MODEL AND REHEARSE.*

3a) Model ending a conversation.

1. Refer students to the Time's-Up Tin visual support.
2. Start talking about something and just keep going until the students start acting bored or they stop paying attention.

3. When the students lose interest, stop your story, and say aloud, "Okay, I see that you are no longer interested in my story. I can tell because you're no longer looking at me, you're moving around in your seats, and you're doing other things. I guess I will wrap it up by saying 'And that's the end.'" Model endings and have students imitate your response. Provide feedback and prompt students to mark their data on Line A of the Self-Monitoring Data Sheet.
4. Ask the students, "What should I do now?" (The students should answer by telling you to wrap up the story or conversation and/or point to the Time's-Up Tin visual support.)

3b) Have the students rehearse ending conversations in pairs.

1. Ask for a volunteer to come up and have a conversation with you in front of the class.
2. So that the other students do not hear, quietly tell the volunteer that after about 30 seconds he or she should begin acting bored by looking around the room, yawning, or looking at the clock.
3. Begin speaking, then when the volunteer begins acting bored, say aloud, "I am thinking about my listener, and I think I know why he [or she] is bored. I wonder what I can do to keep my listener interested."
4. Ask the volunteer a question. If he or she still acts bored, say aloud, "I think [volunteer's name] is done listening. I am going to wrap up this story."
5. End the story with a practiced ending such as "That's it" or "Time to go."
6. Switch roles and have the student be the one that tells the story and needs to end the conversation.
7. Prompt the students to give the speaker clear clues when they want to end the conversation.

3c) Prompt the students to mark their data on Line B of the Self-Monitoring Data Sheet.

I can give the speaker clear feedback to wrap it up

○ by myself ○ with peer help ○ with teacher help

STEP 4. *ROLE-PLAY AND REINFORCE.*

4a) Have the students role-play ending a conversation.

1. Place students in pairs.
2. Direct the students to take turns telling a story and practicing the following steps when their partner begins to act bored:

   —Think about how they can keep the listeners interested.

   —Think about what they can do when the listeners are finished listening.

   —End the story appropriately when their partner is finished listening.
3. Make sure each student has a turn being the listener and speaker.
4. Provide feedback for each student.

4b) Prompt the students to mark their data on Line C of the Self-Monitoring Data Sheet.

I can end interactions successfully in role play

◯ by myself ◯ with peer help ◯ with teacher help

STEP 5. *PROMOTE GENERALIZATION.*

Send home the Parent Follow-Up Page.

Follow-up directions are provided on the Parent Follow-Up Page.

APPENDIX A

PHOTOCOPIABLE MATERIALS FOR USE IN MULTIPLE LESSONS

SOCIAL COMPASS ICONS OVERVIEW

READING COMPREHENSION SHEETS (copying instructions per student)

Module 1 (make 4 copies) 117

Module 2 (make 4 copies) 118

Module 3 (make 7 copies) 119

Module 4 (make 9 copies) 120

SOCIAL COMPASS ICONS OVERVIEW

Body Language Binoculars

Proximity Compass

Voice-o-Meter

Glance Gauge

Emotional Climate Map

Emotional Intensity Indicator

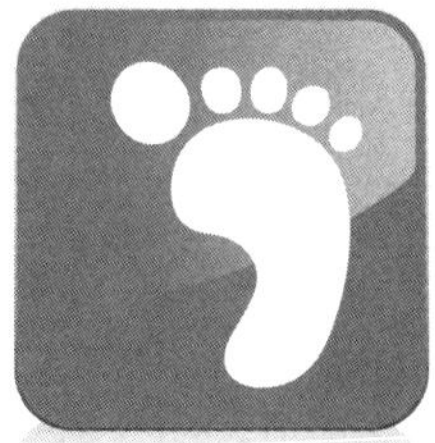
Empathy Footprint

Positive Headset

Relevance Radar

Trail Marker

GPS Alert

Self-Portrait

Handle

Self-Controller

Membership Card

Start Button

Question Bubble

Display Case

Compliment Confetti

Interest Inventory

Paraphrasing Funnel

Friendship Balance

Conversation Glue

Time's-Up Tin

MODULE 1 READING COMPREHENSION SHEET

1. What was the visual support? Select one.

○  ○ 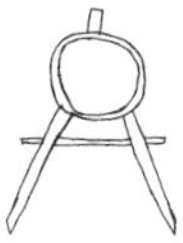 ○  ○ 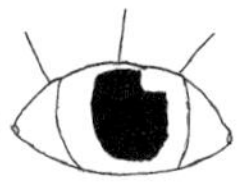

2. Who was the story about? Select one.

○ Brad ○ Spencer ○ Victor ○ Steve

3. What was his problem? Select one.

○ Not looking at speaker ○ Getting too close
○ Talking too loudly ○ Staring too long

4. What did he learn to do about it? Select one.

○ Look at the speaker ○ Speak softly
○ Stand back ○ Stop staring

5. Draw or summarize the story.

MODULE 2 READING COMPREHENSION SHEET

1. What was the visual support? Select one.

○  ○ 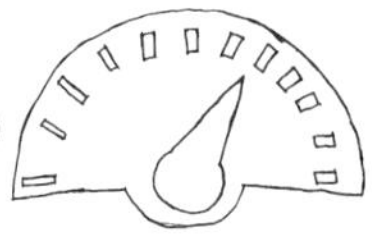 ○  ○ 

2. Who was the story about? Select one.

○ Eddy ○ Ida ○ Emanuel ○ Cory

3. What was his or her problem? Select one.

○ Not managing intense feelings
○ Doesn't know how to show he or she cares about others
○ Being mean to oneself
○ Can't read faces to tell how people are feeling

4. What did he or she learn to do about it? Select one.

○ Read emotions ○ Be nice to oneself
○ Talk about intense feelings ○ Help make people feel better

5. Draw or summarize the story.

MODULE 3 READING COMPREHENSION SHEET

1. What was the visual support? Select one.

○  ○  ○ 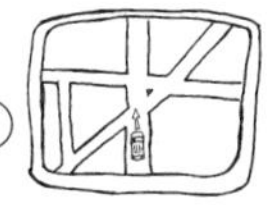 ○ 

○ 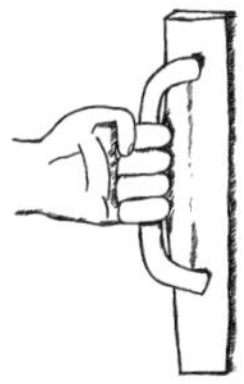 ○ 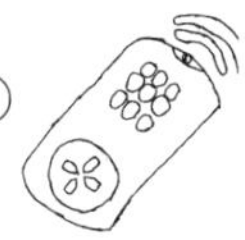 ○ 

2. Who was the story about? Select one.

○ Al ○ Pat ○ Brad ○ Bob ○ Freddy ○ Tanya ○ Ricky

3. What was his or her problem? Select one.

○ Didn't control anger
○ Got upset over a change
○ Didn't listen to the teacher
○ Didn't get included
○ Interrupted the class
○ Didn't know how to handle being teased
○ Focused on others and not on self

4. What did he or she learn to do about it? Write your answer.

5. Draw or summarize the story.

MODULE 4 READING COMPREHENSION SHEET

1. What was the visual support? Select one.

○ 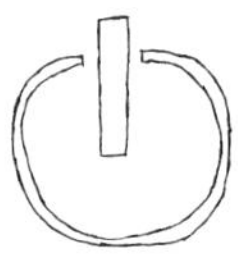 ○  ○ 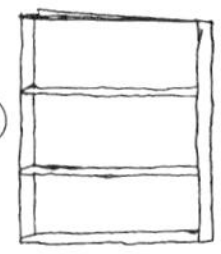 ○  ○ 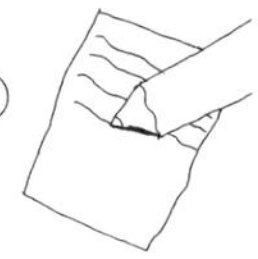

○ 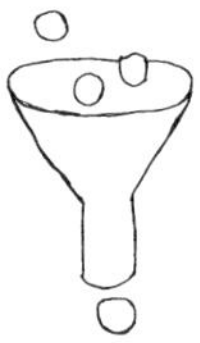 ○  ○  ○ 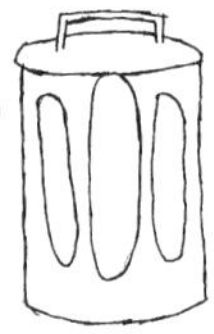

2. Who was the story about? Select one.

○ Willy ○ Evan ○ Connie ○ Alex
○ Sharon ○ Ned ○ Mike ○ Patrick ○ Frank

3. What was his or her problem? Select one.

○ Didn't know how to compliment someone
○ Didn't know when to stop talking
○ Didn't share knowledge with others
○ Didn't know how to start a conversation
○ Didn't give friends a turn to talk
○ Didn't know about things others know
○ Didn't get more information
○ Didn't think about what friends like
○ Didn't seem to listen by checking in with the speaker

4. What did he or she learn to do about it? Write your answer.

5. Draw or summarize the story.

APPENDIX B
LESSON-SPECIFIC RESOURCES

Module 1

Lesson 1A	Self-Monitoring Data Sheet	123
	Handout for Lesson 1A: Gesture Guide	124
	Parent Follow-Up Page	125
Lesson 1B	Self-Monitoring Data Sheet	126
	Handout for Lesson 1B: Proximity Compass and Relationship Rings	127
	Parent Follow-Up Page	128
Lesson 1C	Self-Monitoring Data Sheet	129
	Parent Follow-Up Page	130
Lesson 1D	Self-Monitoring Data Sheet	131
	Parent Follow-Up Page	132

Module 2

Lesson 2A	Self-Monitoring Data Sheet	133
	Parent Follow-Up Page	134
Lesson 2B	Self-Monitoring Data Sheet	135
	Handout for Lesson 2B: Emotional Intensity Indicator	136
	Parent Follow-Up Page	137
Lesson 2C	Self-Monitoring Data Sheet	138
	Parent Follow-Up Page	139
Lesson 2D	Self-Monitoring Data Sheet	140
	Parent Follow-Up Page	141

Module 3

Lesson 3A	Self-Monitoring Data Sheet	142
	Parent Follow-Up Page	143
Lesson 3B	Self-Monitoring Data Sheet	144
	Parent Follow-Up Page	145
Lesson 3C	Self-Monitoring Data Sheet	146
	Parent Follow-Up Page	147
Lesson 3D	Self-Monitoring Data Sheet	148
	Parent Follow-Up Page	149
Lesson 3E	Self-Monitoring Data Sheet	150
	Parent Follow-Up Page	151
Lesson 3F	Self-Monitoring Data Sheet	152
	Parent Follow-Up Page	153
Lesson 3G	Self-Monitoring Data Sheet	154
	Parent Follow-Up Page	155

Module 4

Lesson 4A	Self-Monitoring Data Sheet	156
	Handout for Lesson 4A: List of Topics for Starting a Conversation	157
	Parent Follow-Up Page	158

Lesson 4B	Self-Monitoring Data Sheet	159
	Parent Follow-Up Page	160
Lesson 4C	Self-Monitoring Data Sheet	161
	Handout for Lesson 4C: Interest Inventory	162
	Parent Follow-Up Page	163
Lesson 4D	Self-Monitoring Data Sheet	164
	Parent Follow-Up Page	165
Lesson 4E	Self-Monitoring Data Sheet	166
	Parent Follow-Up Page	167
Lesson 4F	Self-Monitoring Data Sheet	168
	Parent Follow-Up Page	169
Lesson 4G	Self-Monitoring Data Sheet	170
	Parent Follow-Up Page	171
Lesson 4H	Self-Monitoring Data Sheet	172
	Parent Follow-Up Page	173
Lesson 4I	Self-Monitoring Data Sheet	174
	Parent Follow-Up Page	175

1A SELF-MONITORING DATA SHEET
BODY LANGUAGE/GESTURES

Rate the following behaviors as

1—I did it by myself
2—I did it with peer help
3—I did it with teacher help

A. I can label photos of gestures. Write in label on line:	 __________	 __________	 __________	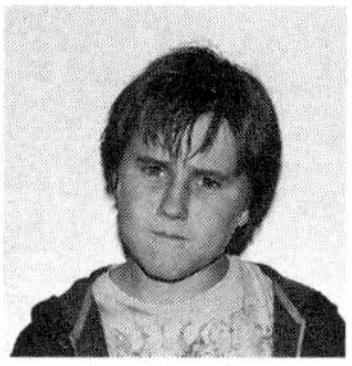 __________
SKILL	**TRIAL 1**	**TRIAL 2**	**TRIAL 3**	**TRIAL 4**
B. I can imitate a variety of facial expressions: sad, angry, happy, scared.				
C. I can role-play gestures from my Body Language Binoculars.				
D. I can respond to a peer's nonverbal behavior in a role play.				

Comments:

1A HANDOUT
GESTURE GUIDE

Just a minute

Over here

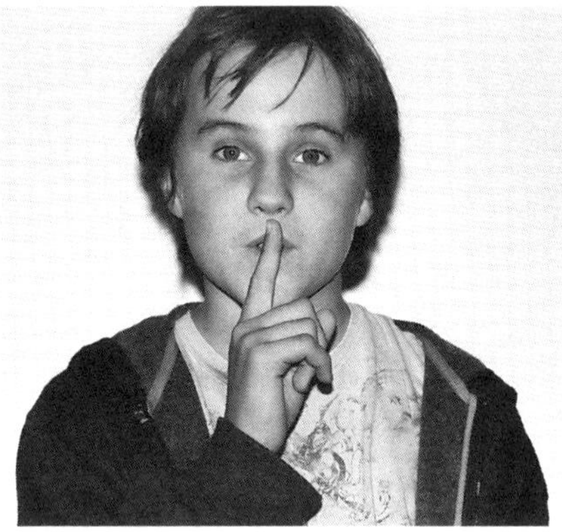

Be quiet

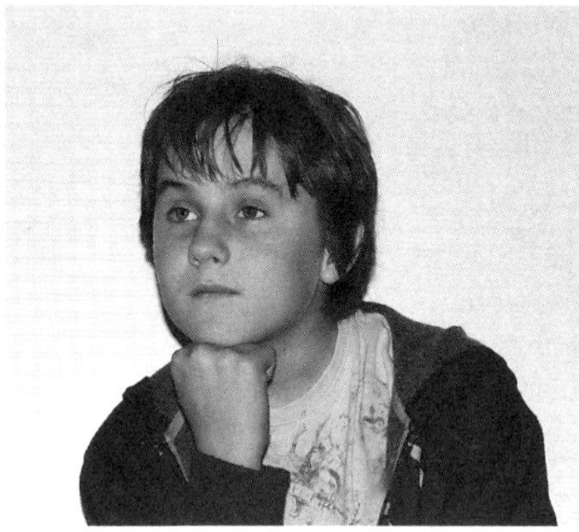

I'm thinking

Wow, I'm surprised

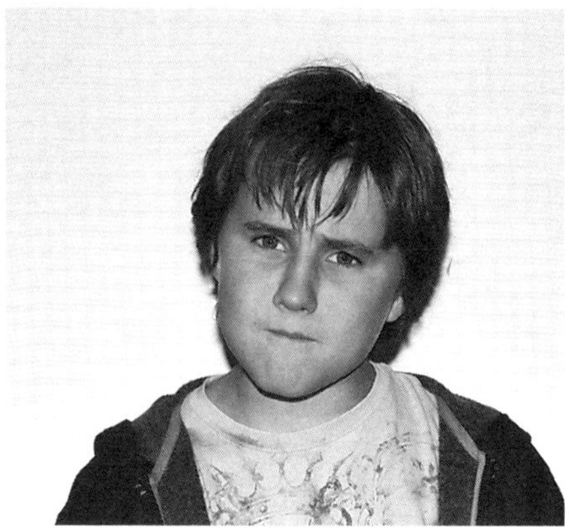

I'm really angry

1A PARENT FOLLOW-UP PAGE
BODY LANGUAGE/GESTURES

Welcome to *The Social Compass Curriculum: A Story-Based Intervention Package for Students with Autism Spectrum Disorders*. This program, like a compass, will help children navigate social situations and understand their emotions. The Parent Follow-Up Page is dedicated to helping you continue practicing your child's target skills at home.

Starting at the top of the compass, or north, this first lesson is part of Module 1: Nonverbal Skills. The target skills for this module incorporate learning how to read someone else's body language and responding appropriately to someone else's body language. Each lesson is structured around a new skill. The skill is described in a Social Compass story, then modeled and practiced through activities in a group. Your job is to keep practicing and reinforcing the skill when you see it being used. The story in this first lesson is about Brad's body language. The strategy he learned was to imagine he saw the situation through his Body Language Binoculars as a whole picture (words plus actions of others) before he responds to a social situation. This week, Brad learned to always look at a person to decide how to speak before responding.

Your task is to create situations that absolutely require your child to look at you to give an appropriate answer. This can be done when giving directions, for example, by saying, "What's this?" then pointing rather than naming the item you are talking about. Another technique is to be vague in your directions (e.g., "Put that one over there."). Be sure to gently guide your child to get to the correct response, and praise or reinforce every job well done. Also, explain to your child why it is helpful for him or her to be able to do this skill.

1B SELF-MONITORING DATA SHEET
SPACE AND PROXIMITY

Rate the following behaviors as

1—I did it by myself
2—I did it with peer help
3—I did it with teacher help

A. I can color in the correct ring for the relationship named in the box.	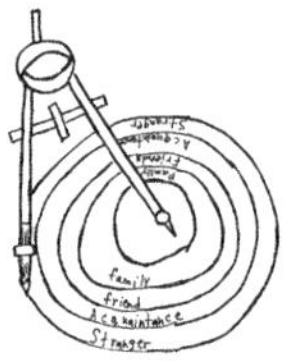 Family	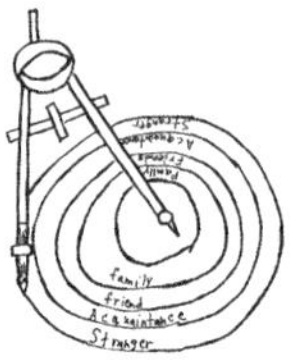 Friend	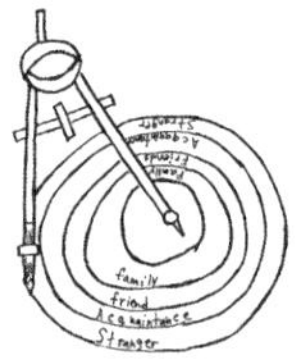 Acquaintance	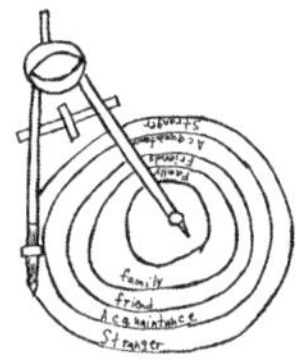 Stranger
SKILL	**TRIAL 1**	**TRIAL 2**	**TRIAL 3**	**TRIAL 4**
B. I can imitate a model on where to stand in relation to another person given the type of relationship.				
C. I can show appropriate distance with a partner in a role-play of his or her choice.				

Comments:

This lesson was inspired by *The Circles Curriculum*, published by James Stanfield Publishing (http://www.stanfield.com/products/family-life-relationships/circles-curriculum).

1B HANDOUT
PROXIMITY COMPASS AND RELATIONSHIP RINGS

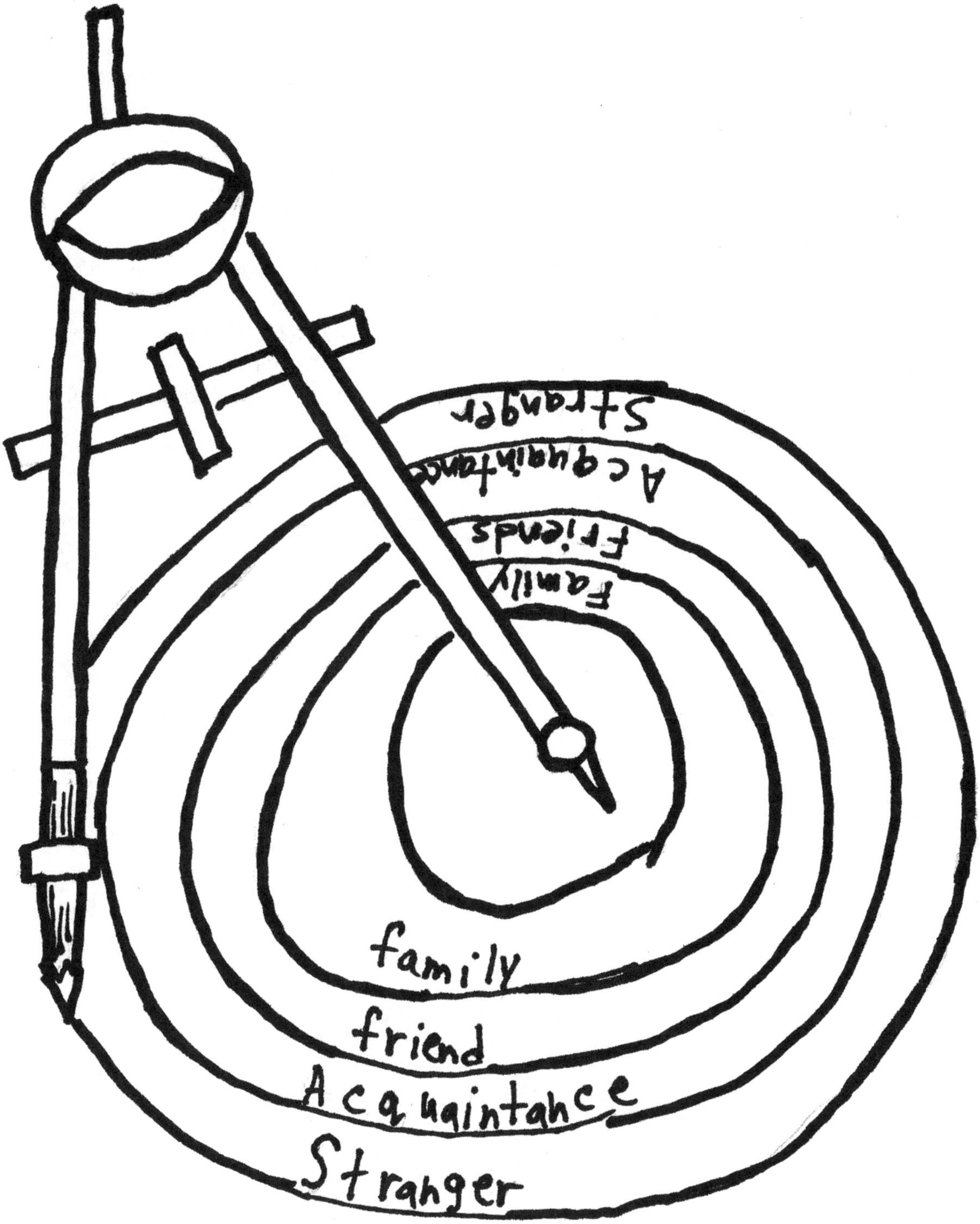

This lesson was inspired by *The Circles Curriculum*, published by James Stanfield Publishing (http://www.stanfield.com/products/family-life-relationships/circles-curriculum).

1B PARENT FOLLOW-UP PAGE
SPACE AND PROXIMITY

This second lesson is also part of Module 1: Nonverbal Skills. The target skill is learning appropriate personal space. The Social Compass story is about Spencer's space. The strategy he learned was to use his Proximity Compass: a compass that draws concentric circles to represent the boundaries of different types of relationships (family, friend, acquaintance, stranger). Each circle represents where someone would stand in relation to the person listed in each circle. The concept for this lesson is inspired by a larger curriculum titled *Circles*, published by the James Stanfield Company. (For more information on this product, visit http://www.stanfield.com/products/family-life-relationships/circles-curriculum.)

In terms of this lesson, help your child practice the concept of personal space and safety by holding up photos of people from the different categories and asking your child to choose the appropriate distance to stand for that photo as if the person were in the room.

Again, be sure to gently guide your child to get to the correct response, and praise every job well done. Also, point out why this is a helpful skill for your child: Understanding appropriate distance to keep between people is important for your child's safety as well as his or her social skills development.

1C SELF-MONITORING DATA SHEET
VOLUME OF VOICE

Rate the following behaviors as

1—I did it by myself
2—I did it with peer help
3—I did it with teacher help

A. I can identify my teacher's or partner's volume and tone.	Whisper	Loud	Happy	Angry
SKILL	**TRIAL 1**	**TRIAL 2**	**TRIAL 3**	**TRIAL 4**
B. I can imitate my teacher's or partner's volume and tone.				
C. I can role-play appropriate tone of voice with a partner for a situation of choice.				

Comments:

1C PARENT FOLLOW-UP PAGE
VOLUME OF VOICE

This lesson is also part of Module 1: Nonverbal Skills. The target skill is understanding appropriate volume of voice. The Social Compass story is about Victor's loud voice. The strategy he learned was to check his imaginary Voice-o-Meter to be sure he matched his voice to the environment.

Remind your child to use an indoor voice when inside and to watch how others react to his or her voice. Some places such as a library or a movie theater require a very quiet voice. Other times, such as at a party or a skating rink, it's okay to be loud.

During this lesson, the students practice measuring how loud they sound to each other by marking the level of volume on the Voice-o-Meter. You can practice this at home by acting out certain scenarios in different settings or just talking about what kind of voice is appropriate for different settings.

As always, be sure to gently guide your child to get to the correct response, and praise every job well done. Also, point out why this is a helpful skill for your child: Knowing when and where to use what volume of voice can help ensure appropriate social exchanges.

1D SELF-MONITORING DATA SHEET
SOCIAL REFERENCING

Rate the following behaviors as

1—I did it by myself
2—I did it with peer help
3—I did it with teacher help

A. I can label staring, glancing, and looking from a model.	Glance	Stare	Look
SKILL	**TRIAL 1**	**TRIAL 2**	**TRIAL 3**
B. I can look at my partner to know when to toss the bean bag based on referencing his or her body language.			
C. I can role-play referencing a group to communicate the desire to join in from the outside of the circle.			

Comments:

1D PARENT FOLLOW-UP PAGE
SOCIAL REFERENCING

This is the last lesson in Module 1: Nonverbal Skills. The target skill is social referencing, or assessing a social situation to understand what's going on. The Social Compass story is about Steve staring. Steve needed to learn that people often look quickly at others to gain information about them and what they're thinking. People also look to figure out how they are expected to act. The strategy Steve learned was to glance at another's eyes to gain quick information (e.g., Is it safe to be near this person? Is he or she trying to communicate with me?). He also learned to acknowledge that he is looking when eye contact is returned. If someone stares at others without adding a gesture or comment, often it becomes uncomfortable and confusing for them. They are looking to understand the individual's intention.

Furthermore, people maintain eye contact to communicate that they want to join in, as noted by the work of Michelle Garcia Winner. Many more in-depth activities can be found in her published works and on her web site (www.socialthinking.com).

To practice this skill at home, try a game of "hot potato." Eye contact with someone begins the game. Look and nod if you want to toss and/or receive the potato, and look to the next person to pass it on.

As always, be sure to gently guide your child to get to the correct response, and praise every job well done. Also, try to point out why this is a helpful skill for your child: Understanding social situations can help your child at school, at play, and at work. It is very helpful to be able to communicate just by exchanging a glance with someone.

2A SELF-MONITORING DATA SHEET
INCREASING EMOTIONAL VOCABULARY

Rate the following behaviors as

1—I did it by myself
2—I did it with peer help
3—I did it with teacher help

A. I can label the correct emotion from a model.	Mad	Sad	Happy	Hurt
SKILL	**TRIAL 1**	**TRIAL 2**	**TRIAL 3**	**TRIAL 4**
B. I can imitate emotional states during a role play.				
C. I can respond to others' emotional states in a role play.				

Comments:

2A PARENT FOLLOW-UP PAGE
INCREASING EMOTIONAL VOCABULARY

Welcome to the first lesson in the second module of *The Social Compass Curriculum.* Moving around the compass clockwise, the next direction is east, so this section includes lessons to help understand emotions. This lesson uses an Emotional Climate Map for the visual support. This first lesson in this module is devoted to identifying emotions in others. In the Social Compass story, Eddy learns about emotional words such as *happy, sad, angry, confused* or *lost,* and *hurt.* The class practiced understanding emotions by looking at pictures of people demonstrating various emotions. The group also practiced shifting emotional states as the situation or social climate changed. Feel free to practice this at home by modeling two emotional states and having your child label them and when you transitioned from one to another.

Your child's homework is to take some time every day to stop and practice identifying emotions in others. It can be on the spot, at home, or with characters on TV. A video recording works well because you can review the emotion by pausing and/or replaying it. Most importantly, focus on providing your child with positive feedback—be sure to reinforce good behavior with praise or something special your child likes. Have fun!

2B SELF-MONITORING DATA SHEET
IDENTIFYING INTENSITY OF FEELINGS

Rate the following behaviors as

1—I did it by myself
2—I did it with peer help
3—I did it with teacher help

A. I can label feelings in modeled examples.	Furious	Happy	Really sad	A little mad
SKILL	**TRIAL 1**	**TRIAL 2**	**TRIAL 3**	**TRIAL 4**
B. I can imitate feelings from the Emotional Intensity Indicator.				
C. I can role-play intense feelings and walk away.				

Comments:

2B HANDOUT
EMOTIONAL INTENSITY INDICATOR

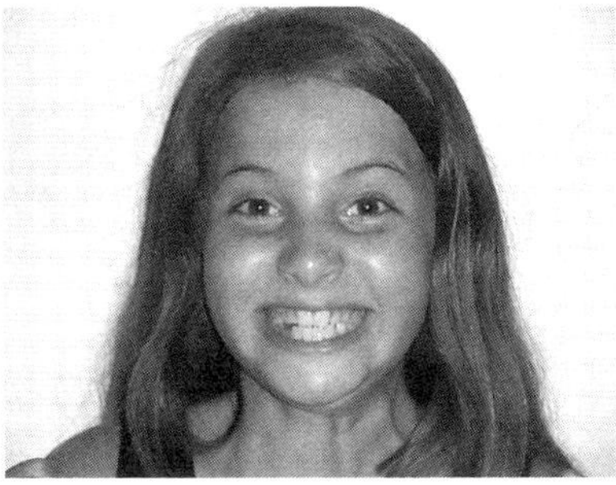

Excited

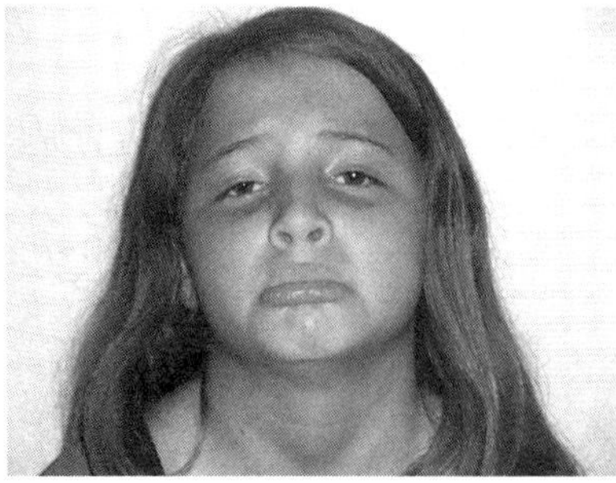

Miserable

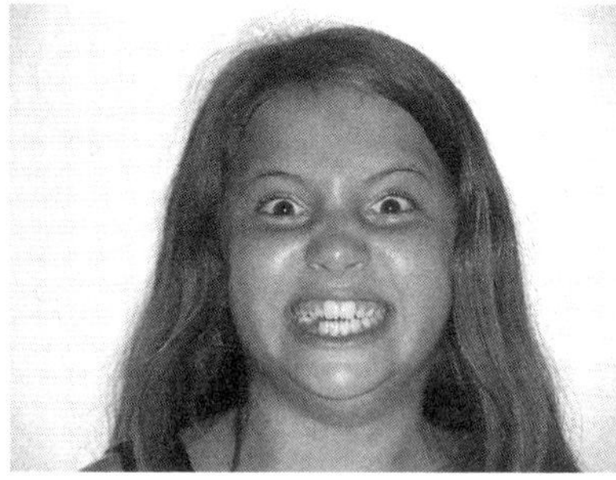

Furious

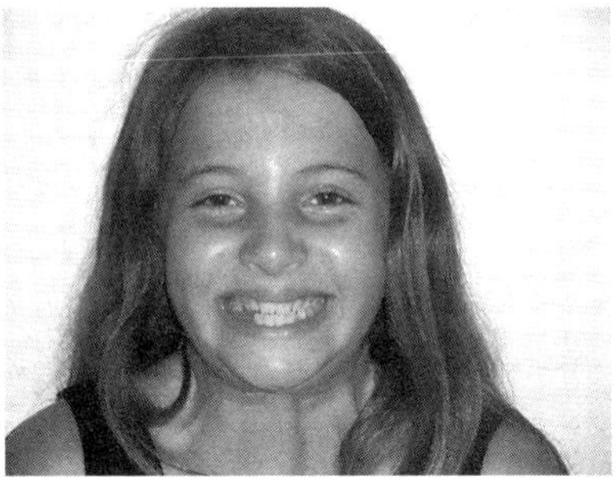

Really happy

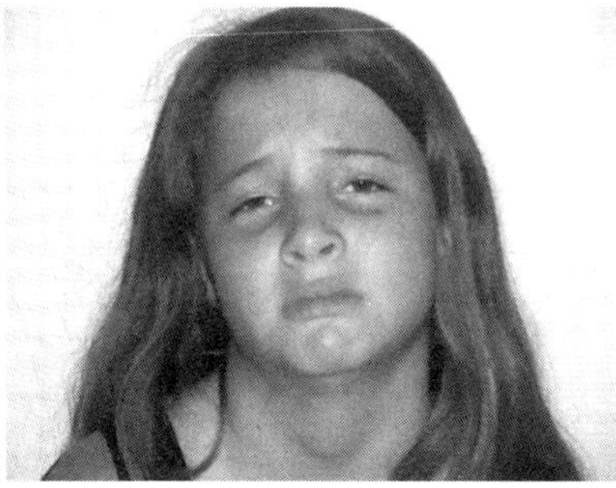

Really sad

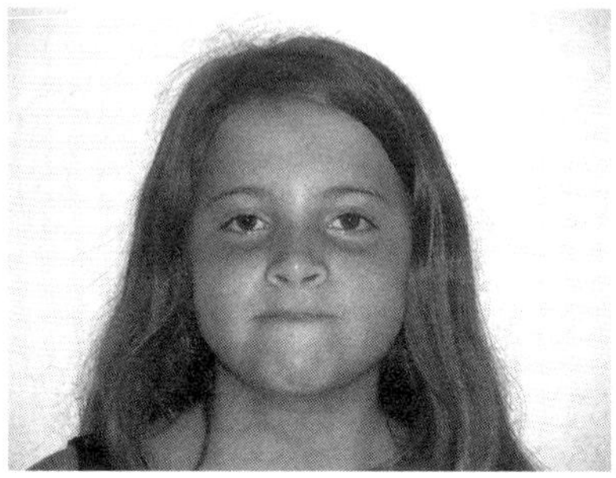

Really mad

Happy

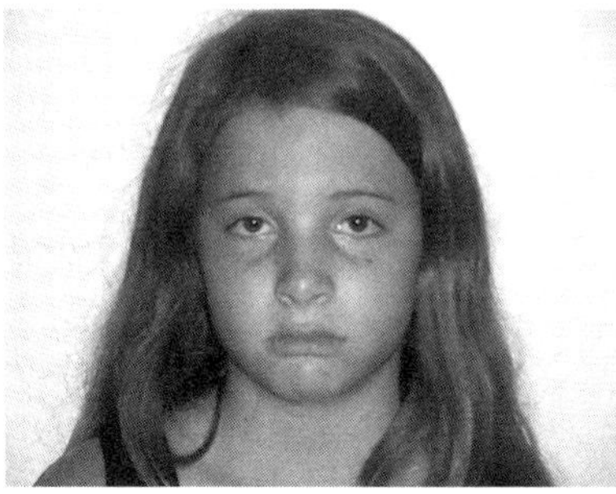

Sad

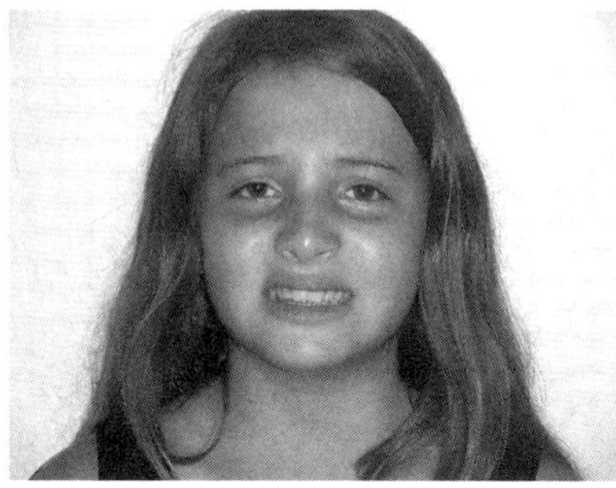

Mad

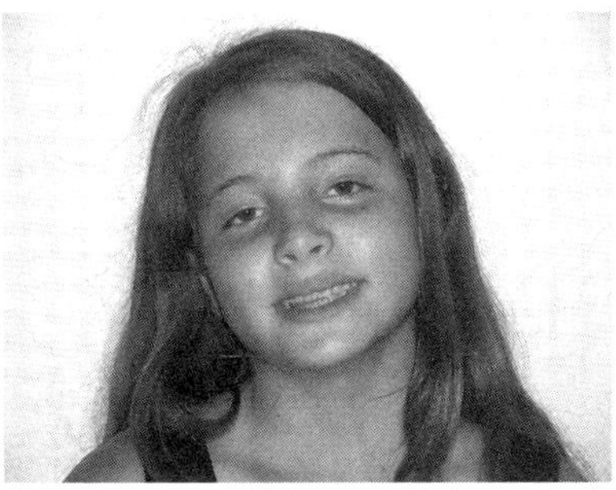

A little happy

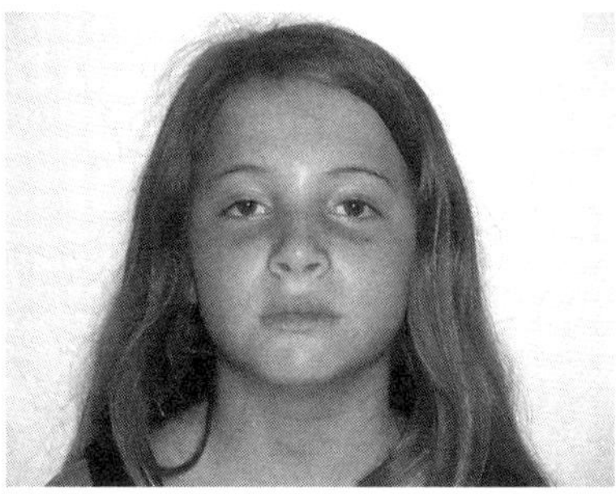

A little sad

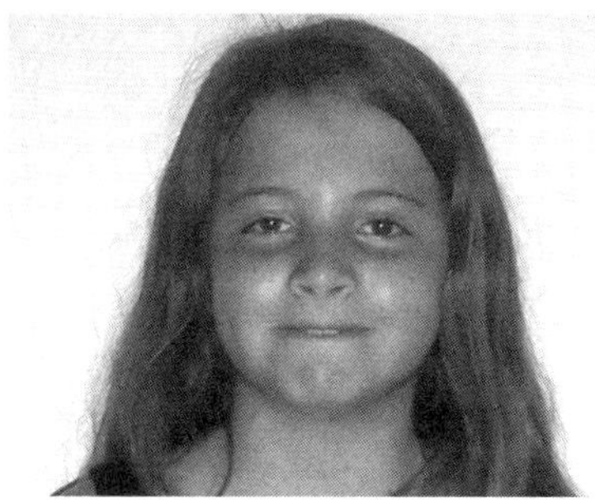

A little mad

2B PARENT FOLLOW-UP PAGE
IDENTIFYING INTENSITY OF FEELINGS

This is the second lesson in Module 2: Emotions. The goal of this lesson is to help students correctly identify intense feelings in oneself and express those intense feelings in an appropriate and safe manner. You can help your child practice this at home. This can be done incidentally by asking your child to rate the intensity of his or her feelings on a scale during any given moment. A word of caution: It is best to begin with positive emotions to be sure your child receives positive feedback right from the start—assuming, that is, that he or she gets the positive emotions correct and has no difficulty discussing them. After developing a positive history for this task, try to catch negative emotions. The act of just interrupting to label the intensity of an emotion may help redirect a high-intensity emotion to a lower state. This may make it easier for your child to process and discuss at some point in time.

If it is too much to catch the emotions live, you can also refer to the TV. Using the television may be easier for your child to master, as it doesn't rely on personal emotion. Remember to stay positive and reward correct responding even if the emotions are negative. And have fun!

2C SELF-MONITORING DATA SHEET
EMPATHY

Rate the following behaviors as

1—I did it by myself
2—I did it with peer help
3—I did it with teacher help

A. I can label correct empathetic statements in stories by circling the right answer.	Story 1 Bob runs over to him and says, "I am so sorry, are you okay?" Jonny says, "Yes, I will be alright in a minute."	Story 2 A girl says to Chris, "Join in." The student keeps running by and says, "Sorry, it was an accident."	Story 3 Brandon shouts at Alex, "Hey, cut it out!" Alex says, "It was an accident!" Brandon tells his coach, and his coach says, "I'm sorry that happened to you; are you okay?"
SKILL	**TRIAL 1**	**TRIAL 2**	**TRIAL 3**
B. I can imitate empathetic statements.			
C. I can role-play empathy for others in a situation of choice.			

Comments:

2C PARENT FOLLOW-UP PAGE
EMPATHY

In this week's lesson, the focus is on learning what empathy is and what it looks like, imitating making empathetic statements, and role-playing examples. The visual support is an Empathy Footprint to symbolize walking in someone else's shoes. The story about Emanuel learning to be empathetic involved him observing his friend get sad, analyzing the movements on his friend's face, and recognizing the feeling. He then took a "step" to help his friend feel better. He went to him to cheer him up.

Your homework is to ask your child to tell you the Social Compass story, or another that he or she is familiar with, in his or her words. Have your child describe the hurt person's feelings and explain how that makes him or her feel or pretend how it would feel if your child cared about that person. Lastly, have your child brainstorm what he or she could do to show support. List things your child could say or do and how that would most likely make the other person feel. Remember to keep it light and fun.

As always, be sure to gently guide your child to get to the correct response, and praise every job well done. Also, point out why this is a helpful skill for your child: Empathy is a cornerstone of friendship, so being able to understand how someone else feels is a great way to connect with people and feel close.

2D SELF-MONITORING DATA SHEET POSITIVE SELF-TALK

Rate the following behaviors as

1—I did it by myself
2—I did it with peer help
3—I did it with teacher help

A. I can label positive and negative self-talk in written statements by circling them.	I am terrible at this!	I am always last!	I will do it better next time!	I will never give up!
SKILL	**TRIAL 1**	**TRIAL 2**	**TRIAL 3**	**TRIAL 4**
B. I can label positive self-talk statements.				
C. I can use positive self-talk in role plays.				

Comments:

2D PARENT FOLLOW-UP PAGE
POSITIVE SELF-TALK

Positive self-talk is a term used to describe the behavior of making positive statements to and about ourselves. This lesson, the last in Module 2: Emotions, is a pivotal one. How individuals talk to themselves can have a significant impact on their feelings and actions. People's thoughts affect their actions, so it is important to have a positive mind-set about life's events. The visual prompt for this lesson is a Positive Headset.

It is important to coach your child to make positive statements about him- or herself. You can prompt your child to make these statements out loud so that you can then reward the positive behavior. Try saying, "You must be proud of yourself" in a situation in which you may have said, "I am proud of you" before.

Watch for accomplishments, and expand your response from what may have been "Good job" to a "Wow, how did that make you feel?" "Wow, you must be proud" or "How do you think you did?" to help your child understand and recognize ways he or she can encourage him- or herself.

Also watch to see if your child's body language matches his or her emotion. When it does, you can start to decrease your prompting and just watch your child's body language. When you see defeated body language, provide a prompt to turn it to a positive statement you make out loud, and have your child repeat it. For example, if your child slumps after losing a game, you can say, "You may've lost this time—better luck next time." Keep it positive. Even when individuals make mistakes, they can acknowledge it and still not to put themselves down. These are precisely the times to work on your child's positive self-talk.

3A SELF-MONITORING DATA SHEET
STAYING ON TOPIC

Rate the following behaviors as

1—I did it by myself
2—I did it with peer help
3—I did it with teacher help

SKILL	TRIAL 1	TRIAL 2	TRIAL 3	TRIAL 4
A. I can label an example of blurting out the answer.				
B. I can identify when a partner resisted blurting out in rehearsal.				
C. I can role-play staying on topic with a peer.				

Comments:

3A PARENT FOLLOW-UP PAGE
STAYING ON TOPIC

This lesson is the first in Module 3: Social Problem Solving, representing the next direction on the Social Compass, south. The visual for this lesson is a Relevance Radar.

In class, your child read a story about a boy who blurted things out without listening for context or relevance in the situation. Practice the following activity at home, and use the Relevance Radar visual support as needed: Instruct your child to listen to you read or sing quietly. Read or sing a common song or poem and then leave out the last word of each phrase. For example, "I pledge allegiance to the ____." Have your child raise his or her hand in the air when he or she knows the missing information or has the urge to blurt something unrelated. If your child makes irrelevant comments, talk about what makes that comment irrelevant, and illustrate where on the radar it falls. Praise related comments. For extra practice, repeat the song/poem with incorrect words at the end and have your child raise his or her hand again. You can also practice this during typical family situations, such as during dinnertime conversations or phone conversations with relatives. Be sure to help your child refer to the Relevance Radar if he or she starts to get away from the appropriate topic of conversation.

3B SELF-MONITORING DATA SHEET
PAYING ATTENTION

Rate the following behaviors as

1—I did it by myself
2—I did it with peer help
3—I did it with teacher help

SKILL	TRIAL 1	TRIAL 2	TRIAL 3	TRIAL 4
A. I played the "Simon Says" game correctly.				
B. I role-played paying attention during a conversation by B1. Looking at the speaker				
B2. Keeping my hands empty				
B3. Keeping my body facing the speaker				

Comments:

3B PARENT FOLLOW-UP PAGE
PAYING ATTENTION

This is the second lesson in Module 3: Social Problem Solving. The goal of this lesson is to help students learn to stay focused on the group. You can help your child practice this at home through role-play and incidentally with prompting. This lesson uses a Trail Marker as the visual support to remind students to stay on track and remain focused on what others around them are doing or discussing.

To set up a role play, tell your child that you want him or her to practice the behaviors that are required in paying attention, such as looking at the speaker, leaning forward, keeping hands free of materials, and nodding occasionally. Tell your child that you are going to begin talking and you want him or her to practice each of the just-mentioned behaviors. You can prompt your child to practice one behavior at a time. It may be helpful to model behaviors associated with paying attention and/or have your child practice in front of a full-length mirror. If there are siblings in the home, you can set up role-play situations between them. To prompt these strategies in a natural situation, try to be aware of your child's listening behaviors throughout the day. If you find that you or someone else is speaking to your child and he or she is not paying attention, remind your child to exhibit one of the listening behaviors he or she has been practicing: looking at the speaker, leaning forward, keeping hands free of materials, and nodding occasionally.

As always, be sure to gently guide your child to get the correct response, and praise every job well done. Also, point out that listening is a helpful skill for your child because it is half of a conversation—it is just as important as speaking. Others are very aware if someone is listening to them speak.

3C SELF-MONITORING DATA SHEET
ACCEPTING CHANGE IN ROUTINES

Rate the following behaviors as

1—I did it by myself
2—I did it with peer help
3—I did it with teacher help

SKILL	TRIAL 1	TRIAL 2	TRIAL 3	TRIAL 4
A. I can label a behavior to cope with change.				
B. I can rehearse making changes in a group game format of musical chairs.				
C. I was able to accept a change in my routine in role play with a peer.				

Comments:

3C PARENT FOLLOW-UP PAGE
ACCEPTING CHANGE IN ROUTINES

This lesson helps students identify why coping with change is important. It is important because change happens so frequently that one needs to be prepared for it. The visual support for this lesson is a GPS Alert. Just as a GPS in a car helps guide the driver through any obstacles to a final destination, the GPS Alert is a reminder for students that a change may occur, but they can get through it.

Practice coping with a change in routine at home by creating changes in the environment (e.g., where family members sit for dinner, which route you take to get to a familiar location—such as a park or the mall). You might want to prepare your child that you're practicing this skill so that he or she can recall the story from class, refer to the visual, and be guided and comforted through the change in routine.

Point to the GPS Alert to indicate for your child that a change is happening and he or she should accept it and move on with the new activity.

As always, be sure to gently guide your child to get the correct response, and praise every job well done. Also, remind your child that changes in routines can happen at any time, but with the right tools and preparation, he or she can be prepared.

3D SELF-MONITORING DATA SHEET RESISTING TATTLING

Rate the following behaviors as

1—I did it by myself
2—I did it with peer help
3—I did it with teacher help

A. Write in the correct answer: 1a. Tell the teacher. 1b. Ignore it and focus on you. 1c. Tell the student the classroom rules.	Story 1 A classmate is eating her snack too early. __________	Story 2 An older student hurt someone on the play-ground. __________	Story 3 A classmate is not reading his book during reading time. __________	Story 4 A student is picking her nose. __________
SKILL	**TRIAL 1**	**TRIAL 2**	**TRIAL 3**	**TRIAL 4**
B. I can rehearse resisting tattling by raising my hand when an opportunity for tattling occurred.				
C. I can role-play not tattling during a structured activity.				

Comments:

3D PARENT FOLLOW-UP PAGE
RESISTING TATTLING

The visual support for this lesson is a Self-Portrait. This helps remind the students to stay focused on themselves and avoid telling on someone else unnecessarily. The Social Compass story for this lesson was about a girl who was a bit nosy and told the teacher on a classmate who wrote down a wrong answer. Students need to know the difference between keeping to oneself for minor infractions and telling an adult for serious situations, such as someone getting hurt or running away.

Assign a family member to engage in an undesired behavior, such as talking too loudly over the TV show being watched. While this behavior is occurring, read a story out loud to your child. Remind your child to hold up his or her hand as a reminder to resist tattling. As your child stays focused on his or her own activity of reading a story, identify the positive response, and praise him or her.

3E SELF-MONITORING DATA SHEET
HANDLING TEASING

Rate the following behaviors as

1—I did it by myself
2—I did it with peer help
3—I did it with teacher help

SKILL	TRIAL 1	TRIAL 2	TRIAL 3	TRIAL 4
A. I can label good responses to teasing.				
B. I can use scripts to handle teasing.				
C. I can use my own statements to handle teasing.				

Comments:

3E PARENT FOLLOW-UP PAGE
HANDLING TEASING

This lesson is intended to help your child avoid hurt feelings from teasing. The visual support for this lesson is a Handle to represent getting a grip and holding on to one's emotions.

Part of this lesson is to recognize if teasing is meant to be friendly and not hurtful. The definition of friendly teasing is when everyone laughs, including most specifically the person being targeted. The other part of this lesson is deciding how to respond to the teasing. Verbal responses such as "That's not funny" or "I don't get it" are appropriate, as are nonverbal responses such as walking away. Your child might also choose to join in the teasing by saying something such as, "Yeah, you're right, my hair does look bad today," and just chuckling along with friends. Often, teasing can be managed by interpreting the comments as friendly and going along with it.

A straightforward role play of teasing each other and responding in a friendly or more direct way is the homework for this lesson. This may be a perfect lesson to have siblings join in; just be sure that everyone knows this is for practice and what topics might be too sensitive for your child. Teaching your child to "get a grip" when teasing is friendly is an important skill to have, especially as the teenage years approach. Being able to let things roll off one's back is an important skill for young people to have.

3F SELF-MONITORING DATA SHEET
USING SELF-CONTROL

Rate the following behaviors as

1—I did it by myself
2—I did it with peer help
3—I did it with teacher help

SKILL	TRIAL 1	TRIAL 2	TRIAL 3	TRIAL 4
A. I can identify angry behaviors modeled by the teacher.				
B. I can rehearse being angry without displaying aggressive behavior.				
C. I can role-play a conflict without losing control and make a positive choice to resolve it.				

Comments:

3F PARENT FOLLOW-UP PAGE
USING SELF-CONTROL

This lesson teaches the students to monitor their own out-of-control behavior in the moment and stop it, slow down, and proceed when they are calm. The visual support for this lesson is a Self-Controller remote control with buttons to stop, slow down, and proceed. This behavior may require repeated modeling by adults in role-play situations. Be sure to label examples of individuals catching themselves and controlling their behavior in your everyday experiences (e.g., if a parent comes home after a bad day at work, you can refer to the Self-Controller as a reminder to look at the situation and take the steps to calm down before reacting).

When your child is ready, take turns role-playing being upset by an incident and recovering or maintaining your self-control. Be sure to reward this behavior, even if the situation seems not to warrant losing control in the first place. This can be a difficult skill to learn, and every success should be noted. By focusing on the recovery or maintenance of one's self-control, you are modeling a positive behavior yourself. The more natural reinforcement that exists in your child's environment, the easier it will be for your child to use this skill on his or her own.

3G SELF-MONITORING DATA SHEET
AVOIDING BEING LEFT OUT

Rate the following behaviors as

1—I did it by myself
2—I did it with peer help
3—I did it with teacher help

SKILL	TRIAL 1	TRIAL 2	TRIAL 3	TRIAL 4
A. I can label behaviors modeled that show how to avoid being left out.				
B. In a game format I can work with others to avoid being left out.				
C. I can role-play becoming part of a group.				

Comments:

3G PARENT FOLLOW-UP PAGE
AVOIDING BEING LEFT OUT

This last lesson in Module 3: Social Problem Solving is devoted to helping students learn how to avoid being left out of a group or activity. The visual support is a Membership Card, a symbol of belonging to a group. Belonging to a group requires repeated positive interactions. Often students get left out based on previous actions of which they may not even be aware or able to remember. Sustaining appropriate behavior naturally leads to being included in groups.

To practice the actions that lead to inclusion at home, play "king or queen for the moment." To play this game, write the names of everyone present on separate scraps of paper, and fold them up. Place the names in a bowl and randomly select a "king" or "queen." The person who is the king or queen in that moment may give everyone an order that can be completed within 15 seconds. Use your judgment to set rules as needed for your family. Some examples may be to put everyone's dishes away, to carry dirty laundry to the laundry basket, or simply to clap hands. Make a note of how everyone feels about the order given, and have the king or queen rate his or her feelings, too. Repeat the game as often as desired. The idea is that the king or queen comes to experience and identify how it feels to be part of the family "kingdom" under each person's rule. At the end of a round, have family members vote for who they would make king or queen. Discuss with your child why the votes go the way they do.

Another option to help your child practice avoiding being left out is to make your own membership card for each person in your family. House rules can be developed, too.

4A SELF-MONITORING DATA SHEET INITIATING A CONVERSATION

Rate the following behaviors as

1—I did it by myself
2—I did it with peer help
3—I did it with teacher help

SKILL	TRIAL 1	TRIAL 2	TRIAL 3	TRIAL 4
A. I can indicate when a model has joined a conversation.				
B. I can practice starting a conversation verbally or with a visual support.				
C. I can start a conversation during a role play within 5 seconds.				

Comments:

4A HANDOUT
LIST OF TOPICS FOR STARTING A CONVERSATION

What did you do this weekend?

Where are you from?

Do you have any brothers or sisters?

What is your favorite food?

Have you seen [movie title] yet?

Do you have any pets?

Where did you get that hat [or those shoes]?

What was the last book you read?

What is your favorite mode of transportation?

If you could travel anywhere in the world, where would you go?

4A PARENT FOLLOW-UP PAGE
INITIATING A CONVERSATION

Welcome to the fourth and last module of *The Social Compass Curriculum*. With the compass pointing west, the "We" Skills module is focused on conversation skills. The first of these skills is initiating a conversation. This curriculum assumes that children are building upon each lesson they learn. For this module in particular, it is important that students have learned the nonverbal skills for entering a group that were covered in Module 1 (understanding body language, proximity, and social referencing) before moving on to lessons in this module. It is assumed that the skills practiced in the first two modules are in the student's repertoire and being used in daily life, at home, and in school.

The skill for this lesson is being able to get involved with conversations and activities. The visual support is a Start Button, in which the physical act of touching the start button to turn on a device is the cue to start talking in a conversation.

At home you can practice having your child initiating a conversation by standing in a group and taking turns having family and friends walk up and join the group. There are numerous situations in which this skill can be practiced. The reward for this practice session is a natural reward: being welcomed by the group! Be sure to welcome each other in a clear and positive manner. Have fun.

4B SELF-MONITORING DATA SHEET
ASKING QUESTIONS

Rate the following behaviors as

1—I did it by myself
2—I did it with peer help
3—I did it with teacher help

SKILL	TRIAL 1	TRIAL 2	TRIAL 3	TRIAL 4
A. I can identify a question to ask a model.				
B. I can recall information about others to ask them a follow-up question.				
C. I can role-play appropriate conversation questions with a partner.				

Comments:

4B PARENT FOLLOW-UP PAGE
ASKING QUESTIONS

This is the second lesson in Module 4: "We" Skills. The goal of this lesson is to help students learn to ask questions during a conversation in order to be a part of it. The story from class was about a boy who talked about what he wanted to talk about, without stopping to ask questions or engage others around him. You can help your child practice asking questions at home. You can do this incidentally as your child engages in a conversation with you or someone else at home.

Remind your child to ask questions based on

1. Current social cues—things that are readily observable about a person
2. Information about a person that is previously known

If there are siblings in the home, you may want to set up role-play situations and have your child practice these strategies. When role-playing a conversation, a good rule is to maintain it for at least three exchanges between participants. Be sure your child understands that questions relevant to the current conversation are appropriate.

As always, be sure to gently guide your child to get the correct response, and praise every job well done. Asking questions is a skill that will be used throughout an individual's life, so be sure to practice this regularly.

Also, point out why this is a helpful skill for your child. For example, explain that asking questions is a great way to learn new information and also shows others you are paying attention to them and are interested in them or what they have to say.

4C SELF-MONITORING DATA SHEET
SHARING INFORMATION

Rate the following behaviors as

1—I did it by myself
2—I did it with peer help
3—I did it with teacher help

A. Circle your interests.	Animals Art Movies Reading Shopping Sleeping Television	Dancing Listening to music Outdoor activities Singing Sports Writing	Board games Cooking Eating Math Playing an instrument Science Sewing	Computers Gardening Museums Playing cards Playing video games Talking to friends
SKILL	**TRIAL 1**	**TRIAL 2**	**TRIAL 3**	**TRIAL 4**
B. I can generate a unique piece of personal information to share.				
C. I can role-play sharing information about myself in a conversation with a peer.				

Comments:

4C HANDOUT INTEREST INVENTORY

Area of interest	Check if interested
Animals	
Art	
Baking	
Board games	
Computers	
Cooking	
Dancing	
Eating	
Gardening	
Listening to music	
Math	
Movies	
Museums	
Outdoor activities	
Playing an instrument	
Playing cards	
Playing video games	
Reading	
Science	
Sewing	
Shopping	
Singing	
Sleeping	
Sports	
Talking to friends	
Television	
Writing	

4C PARENT FOLLOW-UP PAGE SHARING INFORMATION

This lesson helps students learn to share their interests with others. The class read the story "Sharon Shares Her Thoughts" and practiced sharing personal interests with other students. The visual support for this story is a Display Case, which reminds students that it is good to let others know their interests so new connections can occur.

Sharing personal interests contributes to getting to know others and it can feel good too. Sharing information helps glue a conversation and friendship together. We add information about others to our memory, and that helps us make a connection to them. To practice at home, you can draw a display case or simply make a list of each family member's favorite things. Take turns talking about something on each person's list.

4D SELF-MONITORING DATA SHEET
GIVING COMPLIMENTS

Rate the following behaviors as

1—I did it by myself
2—I did it with peer help
3—I did it with teacher help

SKILL	TRIAL 1	TRIAL 2	TRIAL 3	TRIAL 4
A. I can identify why complimenting is important.				
B. I can generate compliments in structured play.				
C. I can role-play giving and receiving compliments in a conversation with a partner.				

Comments:

4D PARENT FOLLOW-UP PAGE
GIVING COMPLIMENTS

Complimenting is a skill that promotes positive relationships between people. Compliments can be used to start a conversation, repair a conversation in trouble, or simply make a social connection with someone. The visual for this lesson is Compliment Confetti—sharing nice things about another is a way to add sparkle to a conversation.

The homework for this lesson is to play "compliment countdown." Place a handful of coins in the center of your group. Assign a number on a die to each member (e.g., 1 is for Mom, 2 is for Dad, 3 is for Child 1, 4 is for Child 2, 5 and 6 are "roll again"). Have youngest member roll first. Have the player who rolls the die give a compliment to the person assigned to the number he or she rolls. If the player does this without any cues, the player gets to take a coin from the middle. Continue playing until all of the coins are taken. Coins can then go into a piggy bank and be a reminder of how much complimenting can "pay off."

4E SELF-MONITORING DATA SHEET
EXPANDING PERSONAL INTERESTS

Rate the following behaviors as

1—I did it by myself
2—I did it with peer help
3—I did it with teacher help

SKILL	TRIAL 1	TRIAL 2	TRIAL 3	TRIAL 4
A. I can recall five of my interests from my Interest Inventory.				
B. I can identify a possible new interest that the teacher has that is different from any of my interests.				
C. I can identify a possible new interest from my interaction with someone in the group.				

Comments:

4E PARENT FOLLOW-UP PAGE
EXPANDING PERSONAL INTERESTS

Expanding personal interests is a lifelong skill. The visual for this lesson is a checklist of interests called the Interest Inventory. It represents an ever-growing list of personal interests. A personal inventory suggests that there is a mental mechanism for measuring one's breadth of knowledge and self-improvement. As interests grow, listening and participating in conversations with others becomes more rewarding. Having a wide range of interests can make having conversations easier.

Help your child think about some things he or she is interested in, then come up with a list of friends and family to talk to find out what they're interested in. Grandparents, aunts, or neighbors can be great resources, and the meetings don't have to be in person to learn more about someone. Using the Interest Inventory visual support, remind your child to check off each person's interests as he or she interviews the people on the list. As people share their interests, encourage your child to respond and share his or her level of interest in that topic. Be a model for your child by choosing positive language for conveying your message. For example, if someone says he or she is interested in a topic that is not pleasant for your child, you can model a response such as "That's interesting," "You seem very knowledgeable about that topic," or "I haven't had that experience; tell me more." Praise your child for participating in this activity.

4F SELF-MONITORING DATA SHEET
PARAPHRASING

Rate the following behaviors as

1—I did it by myself
2—I did it with peer help
3—I did it with teacher help

SKILL	TRIAL 1	TRIAL 2	TRIAL 3	TRIAL 4
A. I can identify the key components of the teacher's story.				
B. I can paraphrase with a correct pronoun in a structured game of Simon Says.				
C. I can paraphrase in a conversation with a partner.				

Comments:

4F PARENT FOLLOW-UP PAGE
PARAPHRASING

This lesson provides a strategy to demonstrate that someone is actively listening and understanding what another person is saying. Paraphrasing is saying back to people a summary of what they have said to you. This lets them know you are listening and understanding. The visual support for this lesson is a Paraphrasing Funnel, which demonstrates that information from a speaker goes in the top and distilled information comes out the bottom from the listener. A funnel has a large opening that many words can "pour into" and as the funnel narrows, it squeezes the message into a summary statement including only pertinent information. We use our words at the large part and ask students to shrink it down to the essential summary. We use the phrase, "listen and condense."

The Social Compass story for this lesson was about a boy who learned to paraphrase. Picking up on the most pertinent details of someone's speech is imperative to truly understanding his or her message. If you are not correct, it is a perfect opportunity for the speaker to clarify his or her message.

Practice paraphrasing at home by telling a familiar story or reciting a recipe and asking your child for a summary. Be sure your child gets to the main point. You may draw it out with a funnel if needed, crossing out nonessential details and leaving the summary at the bottom. Your child can let you practice, too. If you need to clarify, have your child paraphrase your clarification so that he or she knows what you meant and has a chance to be praised for it. Seeking clarification is a crucial part of having a conversation.

This skill is advanced and may take many repetitions to make the concept clear to your child. Mastery of this skill may take much longer, but it is important at school, at home, and at work.

4G SELF-MONITORING DATA SHEET NEGOTIATING NEEDS

Rate the following behaviors as

1—I did it by myself
2—I did it with peer help
3—I did it with teacher help

SKILL	TRIAL 1	TRIAL 2	TRIAL 3	TRIAL 4
A. I can suggest a way to balance the group's choice.				
B. I can role-play negotiating my wants with another person's wants.				

Comments:

4G PARENT FOLLOW-UP PAGE
NEGOTIATING NEEDS

This lesson is about finding a balance between one's own needs and wants against the needs and wants of one's friends. Although it is desirable to stand up for what one wants and needs, it is also valuable to be able to negotiate wants and needs to keep friends happy as well. Finding the balance between these is the goal of this lesson. The visual support is a Friendship Balance to remind students to keep it even.

Rehearse this skill at home with your child by discussing different activities or routines that can be negotiated so that everyone gets something he or she wants. It can be as simple as who gets to pick a movie to watch first, which dessert will be served tonight versus tomorrow night, or what family activity will happen on the weekend. Some scripts to prompt your child to reach closure with this task include the following:

- We'll do it your way this time and my way next time.
- We'll do it your way for a little while.
- I'll let you do ____________ if we can go do ____________ afterward.
- Let's do both.
- I'll go do that with you, but I won't ____________.

4H SELF-MONITORING DATA SHEET MAINTAINING A CONVERSATION

Rate the following behaviors as

1—I did it by myself
2—I did it with peer help
3—I did it with teacher help

SKILL	Take turns	Repeat	Nod	Comment
A. I can identify behavior in a model that keeps a conversation going.				
B. I can demonstrate this skill with a peer.				
	TRIAL 1	**TRIAL 2**	**TRIAL 3**	**TRIAL 4**
C. I can maintain a conversation in role play.				

Comments:

4H PARENT FOLLOW-UP PAGE
MAINTAINING A CONVERSATION

The goal of this lesson is to help students learn how to maintain a conversation in an effective manner. The visual for this lesson is Conversation Glue, and the lesson in class featured ways to hold a conversation together, such as paying attention, nodding, asking questions, and looking at the other person.

You can help your child practice this skill at home. You can do this incidentally as your child begins to talk about his or her favorite topic. You can remind your child to use the following strategies:

Taking turns: Make a few statements and then stop to let the other person make a few statements.
Repeating: Every so often, repeat back parts of what the other person says.
Nodding: Nod to show agreement or understanding of what the other person says.
Commenting: Add your feedback about what is being said.

For extra practice, you can set up role-play situations and have your child practice the strategies just mentioned. When role-playing a conversation, remember that an ideal goal is to maintain it for three exchanges between participants. Prompt your child to refer to the Conversation Glue visual support if he or she needs a reminder to stick to the conversation.

As always, be sure to gently guide your child to get the correct response, and praise every job well done. Also, point out why this is a helpful skill for your child: He or she will always need to know how to keep a conversation going!

41 SELF-MONITORING DATA SHEET
ENDING A CONVERSATION

Rate the following behaviors as

1—I did it by myself
2—I did it with peer help
3—I did it with teacher help

SKILL	TRIAL 1	TRIAL 2	TRIAL 3	TRIAL 4
A. I can imitate practiced endings.				
B. I can give the speaker clear feedback to wrap it up.				
C. I can end interactions successfully in role play.				

Comments:

41 PARENT FOLLOW-UP PAGE
ENDING A CONVERSATION

This is the last lesson of Module 4: "We" Skills. The goal of this lesson is to help students learn how to end a conversation. The Social Compass story was about Willy "wrapping up," or ending, a conversation. The visual support for this lesson is a Times-Up Tin. Just as trash needs to be cleaned up and thrown away when we're done with things, all pieces to a conversation need to be tied up and disposed of when people are ready to wrap up. Willy learned to think about these things when wrapping up a conversation:

- Think about the listeners; are they done listening?
- Are you finished talking?
- Is it time to wrap up?
- How can you neatly end your conversation?

To practice ending a conversation at home, have your child begin telling you about something he or she is highly interested in. When your child has continued talking too long, begin to act bored by looking around the room, moving, or looking at your watch. You may want to prompt your child by saying aloud, "You've been talking a long time, and I am beginning to think about other things. I am not really listening anymore. What could you do to make me still interested in your story?" You can prompt your child to ask you a question. If he or she continues the story, say aloud, "I'm all done listening; what should you do?" Remind your child to "wrap it up."

It may be helpful in the beginning to set up these situations a few times a week. It is also important to look for opportunities to guide your child in using these strategies in real-life situations.

INDEX

Figures are indicated by *f*.

Accepting Change in Routines, 55-58, 146-147
Alternate answers on worksheets, 6
Anger, controlling, 67-70
Applied behavior analysis, 3
ASDs, *see* Autism spectrum disorders
Asking Questions, 81-84, 159-160
Autism Social Skills Profile (ASSP), 5
Autism spectrum disorders (ASDs), 1, 2-3

Being left out, avoiding, 71-74, 154-155
Blurting behavior, avoiding, 47-50
Body Language Binoculars, 11-14
Body Language/Gestures, 11-14, 123-125
Bullying, 63

Centers for Disease Control and Prevention, 2-3
Change in routines, accepting, 55-58, 146-147
Compliment Confetti, 89
"Compliment countdown" game, 165
Complimenting others, 89-92, 164-165
Conversation Glue, 105
Conversation skills
  Asking Questions, 81-84, 159-160
  Ending Conversations, 109-114, 174-175
  Expanding Personal Interests, 93-96, 166-167
  Giving Compliments, 89-92, 164-165
  Initiating Conversations, 77-80, 156-158
  Maintaining a Conversation, 105-108, 172-173
  Negotiating Needs, 101-104, 170-171
  overview, 75
  Paraphrasing, 97-100, 168-169
  Sharing Information, 85-88, 161-163

Display Case, 85

Education initiatives, 4
Emotional Climate Map, 29
Emotional Intensity Indicator tool, 33, 35, 136
Emotional vocabulary, increasing, 29-32, 133-134
Emotions
  controlling anger, 67-70
  Empathy, 37-40, 138-139
  Identifying Intensity of Feelings, 33-36, 135-137
  Increasing Emotional Vocabulary, 29-32, 133-134
  overview, 27
  Positive Self-Talk, 41-43, 140-141
Empathy, 37-40, 138-139
Empathy Footprint, 37
Ending Conversations, 109-114, 174-175
Expanding Personal Interests, 93-96
Eye contact, 23-26, 132

Friendship Balance tool, 101

Games
  "compliment countdown" game, 165
  "king or queen for the moment", 155
  Simon Says, 53, 99
  Social Referencing, 25
Gestures
  context of, 1-2
  lesson on, 11-14, 123-125
Giving Compliments, 89-92, 164-165
Glance Gauge, 23
Goals, by lesson
  Accepting Change in Routines, 55
  Asking Questions, 81
  Avoiding Being Left Out, 71
  Body Language/Gestures, 11
  Empathy, 37
  Ending Conversations, 109
  Expanding Personal Interests, 93
  Giving Compliments, 89
  Handling Teasing, 63
  Identifying Intensity of Feelings, 33
  Increasing Emotional Vocabulary, 29
  Initiating Conversations, 77
  Maintaining a Conversation, 105
  Negotiating Needs, 101
  Paraphrasing, 97
  Paying Attention, 51
  Positive Self-Talk, 41
  Resisting Tattling, 59
  Sharing Information, 85
  Social Referencing, 23
  Space and Proximity, 15
  Staying on Topic, 47
  Using Self-Control, 67
  Volume of Voice, 19
GPS Alert, 55

Handle, 63
Handouts for specific lessons
  Emotional Intensity Indicator, 35, 136
  Gesture Guide, 124
  Interest Inventory, 162
  List of Topics for Starting Conversations, 157
  Proximity Compass and Relationship Rings, 17, 127

Individuals with Disabilities Education Improvement Act (IDEA) of 2004, 4
Information, sharing, 85-88, 161-163
Initiating Conversations, 77-80, 156-158
Intensity of Feelings, Identifying, 33-36, 135-137
Interest Inventory checklist, 93, 162
Interests, expanding personal, 93-96, 166-167

Least restrictive environment (LRE), 4
Left out, avoiding being, 71-74, 154-155
List of Topics for Starting Conversations handout, 157
LRE, *see* Least restrictive environment

Maintaining a Conversation, 105-108, 172-173
Membership Card, 71
Modeling skills
  Accepting Change in Routines, 57-58
  appropriate proximity, 17
  Asking Questions, 83-84
  Avoiding Being Left Out, 73
  Body Language/Gestures, 13
  emotional intensity, 35
  Empathy, 39
  Ending Conversations, 111-112
  Expanding Personal Interests, 95
  Giving Compliments, 91
  Handling Teasing, 65-66
  Increasing Emotional Vocabulary, 31
  Initiating Conversations, 79-80
  Maintaining a Conversation, 107
  Negotiating Needs, 103
  overview, 6
  Paraphrasing, 99-100
  Paying Attention, 53
  Positive Self-Talk, 43
  Resisting Tattling, 61-62
  Sharing Information, 87-88
  Social Referencing, 25
  Staying on Topic, 49-50
  Using Self-Control, 69
  Volume of Voice, 21

Needs, negotiating, 101-104, 170-171
Nonverbal Skills
  Body Language/Gestures, 11-14, 123-125
  gestures, 11-14, 123-125
  overview, 9
  Social Referencing, 23-26, 131-132
  Space and Proximity, 15-18, 126-128
  Volume of Voice, 19-22, 129-130

Paraphrasing, 97-100, 168-169
Paraphrasing Funnel, 97
Parent Follow-Up Pages, by lesson
  Accepting Change in Routines, 147
  Asking Questions, 160
  Avoiding Being Left Out, 155
  Body Language/Gestures, 125
  Empathy, 139
  Ending Conversations, 175
  Expanding Personal Interests, 167
  Giving Compliments, 165
  Handling Teasing, 151
  Identifying Intensity of Feelings, 137
  Increasing Emotional Vocabulary, 134
  Initiating Conversations, 158
  Maintaining a Conversation, 173
  Negotiating Needs, 171
  overview, 6
  Paraphrasing, 169
  Paying Attention, 145
  Positive Self-Talk, 141
  Resisting Tattling, 149
  Sharing Information, 163
  Social Referencing, 132
  Space and Proximity, 128
  Staying on Topic, 143
  Using Self-Control, 153
  Volume of Voice, 130
Paying Attention, 51-54, 144-145
Personal interests, expanding, 93-96, 166-167
PL 108-446, *see* Individuals with Disabilities Education Improvement Act (IDEA) of 2004
Positive Headset, 41
Positive Self-Talk, 41-43, 140-141
Proximity, 15-18, 126-128
Proximity Compass, 15
Proximity Compass and Relationship Rings handout, 17, 127

Question Bubble, 81
Questions, asking, 81-84, 159-160

Reading comprehension sheets, completed examples
  "Al Gets Angry", 68-69
  "Alex Asks Questions", 82-83
  "Blurting Bob", 48-49
  "Brad was a Bully", 72-73
  "Brad's Better Body Language", 12-13
  "Connie Compliments", 90-91
  "Critical Cory", 42
  "Eddy Is Expanding His Emotional Vocabulary", 30-31
  "Emanuel Shows Some Empathy", 38-39
  "Evan's Endless Interests", 94-95
  "Frank Finds the Balance", 102-103
  "Freddy's Friendly Teasing", 65
  "Ida's Story of Intense Feelings", 34
  "Mike Maintains a Conversation", 106-107
  "Ned Gets Nervous", 78-79
  "Pat Likes to Pretend", 52-53
  "Patrick's Paraphrase", 98-99
  "Ricky Rides the Bus", 56-57
  "Sharon Shares Her Thoughts", 86-87
  "Spencer's Space", 16
  "Steve Used to Stare", 24-25
  "Tanya Tries Not to Tattle", 60-61
  "Victor's Loud Voice", 20
  "Willy Wraps It Up", 111
Reading comprehension sheets, overview, 6
Reading comprehension sheets, photocopiable, 117-120
Rehearsing skills
  Accepting Change in Routines, 57-58
  appropriate proximity, 17
  Asking Questions, 83-84
  Avoiding Being Left Out, 73
  Body Language/Gestures, 13
  emotional intensity, 35
  Empathy, 39
  Ending Conversations, 112

Expanding Personal Interests, 95
Giving Compliments, 91
Handling Teasing, 65-66
Increasing Emotional Vocabulary, 31
Initiating Conversations, 79-80
Maintaining a Conversation, 107-108
Negotiating Needs, 103
overview, 6
Paraphrasing, 99-100
Paying Attention, 53
Positive Self-Talk, 43
Resisting Tattling, 61-62
Sharing Information, 87-88
Social Referencing, 25
Staying on Topic, 49-50
Using Self-Control, 69
Volume of Voice, 21
Relevance Radar, 47, 143
Research foundations, of the Social Compass Curriculum
education initiatives, 4
models of research, 3-4
overview, 3
Resisting Tattling, 148-149
Response to intervention (RTI) model, 4, 5*f*
Role plays
Accepting Change in Routines, 58
Asking Questions, 84
Avoiding Being Left Out, 74
Body Language/Gestures, 14
emotional intensity, 35
Empathy, 39-40
Ending Conversations, 112-113
Expanding Personal Interests, 95-96
Giving Compliments, 92
Handling Teasing, 66
Increasing Emotional Vocabulary, 31-32
Initiating Conversations, 80
Maintaining a Conversation, 108
Negotiating Needs, 104
overview, 6
Paraphrasing, 100
Paying Attention, 54
Positive Self-Talk, 43
Resisting Tattling, 62
Sharing Information, 88
Social Referencing, 26
Space and Proximity, 17-18
Staying on Topic, 50
Using Self-Control, 70
Volume of Voice, 21-22
Routines, accepting change in, 55-58, 146-147
RTI model, *see* Response to intervention model

Self-control, 67-70, 152-153
Self-Controller, 67
Self-Monitoring Data Sheets, by lesson
Accepting Change in Routines, 146
Asking Questions, 159
Avoiding Being Left Out, 154
Body Language/Gestures, 123
Empathy, 138
Ending Conversations, 174
Expanding Personal Interests, 166
Giving Compliments, 164
Handling Teasing, 150
Identifying Intensity of Feelings, 135
Increasing Emotional Vocabulary, 133
Initiating Conversations, 156
Maintaining a Conversation, 172
Negotiating Needs, 170
overview, 1, 6
Paraphrasing, 168
Paying Attention, 144
Positive Self-Talk, 140
Resisting Tattling, 148
Sharing Information, 161
Social Referencing, 131
Space and Proximity, 126
Staying on Topic, 142
Using Self-Control, 152
Volume of Voice, 129
Self-Portrait, 59
Self-talk, positive, 41-43, 140-141
Sharing Information, 85-88, 161-163
Simon Says game, 53, 99
Social climate, 7
Social Compass Curriculum
general discussion, 1
instructions for, 5-7
role of teacher feedback in, 1
Social Compass stories
"Al Gets Angry", 67-68
"Alex Asks Questions", 81-82
"Blurting Bob", 47-48
"Brad was a Bully", 71-72
"Brad's Better Body Language", 11-12
"Connie Compliments", 89-90
"Critical Cory", 41-42
"Eddy Is Expanding His Emotional Vocabulary", 29-30
"Emanuel Shows Some Empathy", 37-38
"Evan's Endless Interests", 93-94
"Frank Finds the Balance", 101-102
"Freddy's Friendly Teasing", 63-64
"Ida's Story of Intense Feelings", 33-34
"Mike Maintains a Conversation", 105-106
"Ned Gets Nervous", 77-78
overview, 3
"Pat Likes to Pretend", 51-52
"Patrick's Paraphrase", 97-98
reading and working with, 6
"Ricky Rides the Bus", 55-56
"Sharon Shares Her Thoughts", 85-86
"Spencer's Space", 15-16
"Steve Used to Stare", 23-24
"Tanya Tries Not to Tattle", 59-60
"Victor's Loud Voice", 19-20
"Willy Wraps It Up", 109-110
Social Problem Solving Skills
Accepting Change in Routines, 55-58, 146-147
Avoiding Being Left Out, 71-74, 154-155
Handling Teasing, 63-66, 150-151
overview, 45
Paying Attention, 51-54, 144-145
Resisting Tattling, 59-62, 148-149
Staying on Topic, 47-50, 142-143
Using Self-Control, 67-70, 152-153
Social referencing, 23-26, 131-132
Social skills
essential components in instruction of, 3
impairments, 2-3
Space, 15-18, 126-128
Start Button, 77
Staying on Topic of Conversation, 47-50, 142-143

Tattling, Resisting, 59-62, 148-149
Teasing, handling, 63-66, 150-151
Thoughts, sharing, 85-88, 161-163
Time's-Up Tin, 109
Topic of conversation, paying attention to, 47-50, 142-143
Trail Marker, 51

Visual supports
  benefits of, 4
  overview, 2
  poster and handout, 7
  see also Handouts for specific lessons
Visual supports, by lesson
  Accepting Change in Routines, 55
  Asking Questions, 81
  Avoiding Being Left Out, 71
  Body Language/Gestures, 11
  Empathy, 37
  Ending Conversations, 109
  Expanding Personal Interests, 93
  explaining, 5-6
  Giving Compliments, 89
  Handling Teasing, 63
  Identifying Intensity of Feelings, 33
  Increasing Emotional Vocabulary, 29
  Initiating Conversations, 77
  Maintaining a Conversation, 105
  Negotiating Needs, 101
  Paraphrasing, 97
  Paying Attention, 51
  Positive Self-Talk, 41
  Resisting Tattling, 59
  Sharing Information, 85
  Social Referencing, 23
  Space and Proximity Lesson, 15
  Staying on Topic, 47
  Using Self-Control, 67
  visual icons overview, 116
  Volume of Voice, 19
  see also Handouts for specific lessons
Vocabulary, increasing emotional, 29-32, 133-134
Voice, volume of, 19-22, 129-130
Voice-o-Meter, 19

Wants and needs, balancing, 101-104, 170-171
"We" Skills
  Asking Questions, 81-84, 159-160
  Ending Conversations, 109-114, 174-175
  Expanding Personal Interests, 93-96, 166-167
  Giving Compliments, 89-92, 164-165
  Initiating Conversations, 77-80, 156-158
  Maintaining a Conversation, 105-108, 172-173
  Negotiating Needs, 101-104, 170-171
  overview, 75
  Paraphrasing, 97-100, 168-169
  Sharing Information, 85-88, 161-163